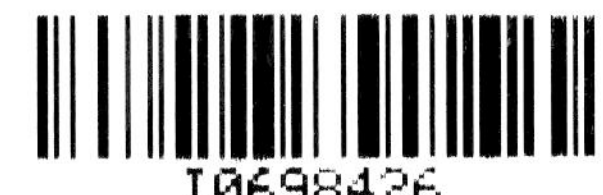

This Coloring book belongs to

....

....

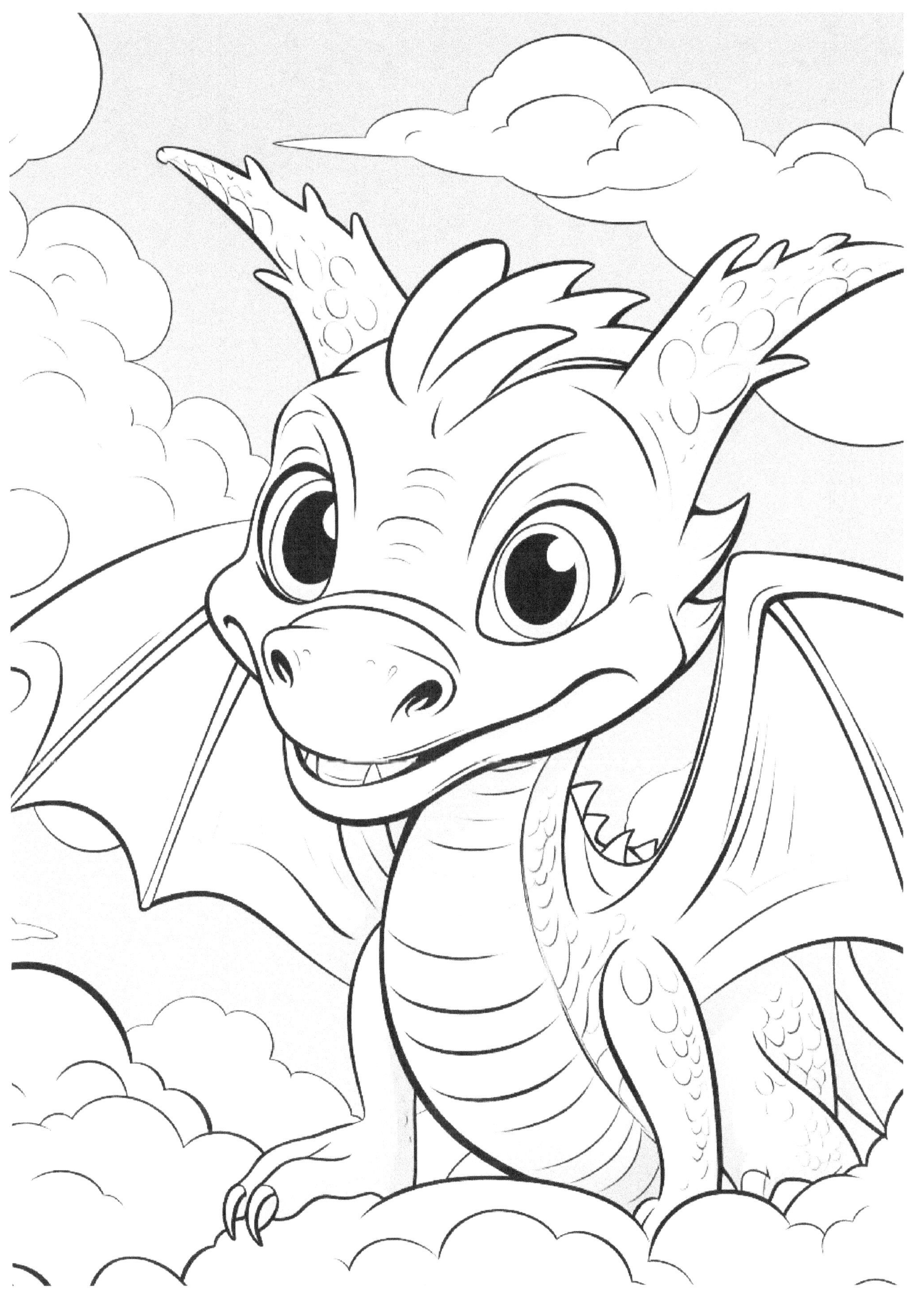

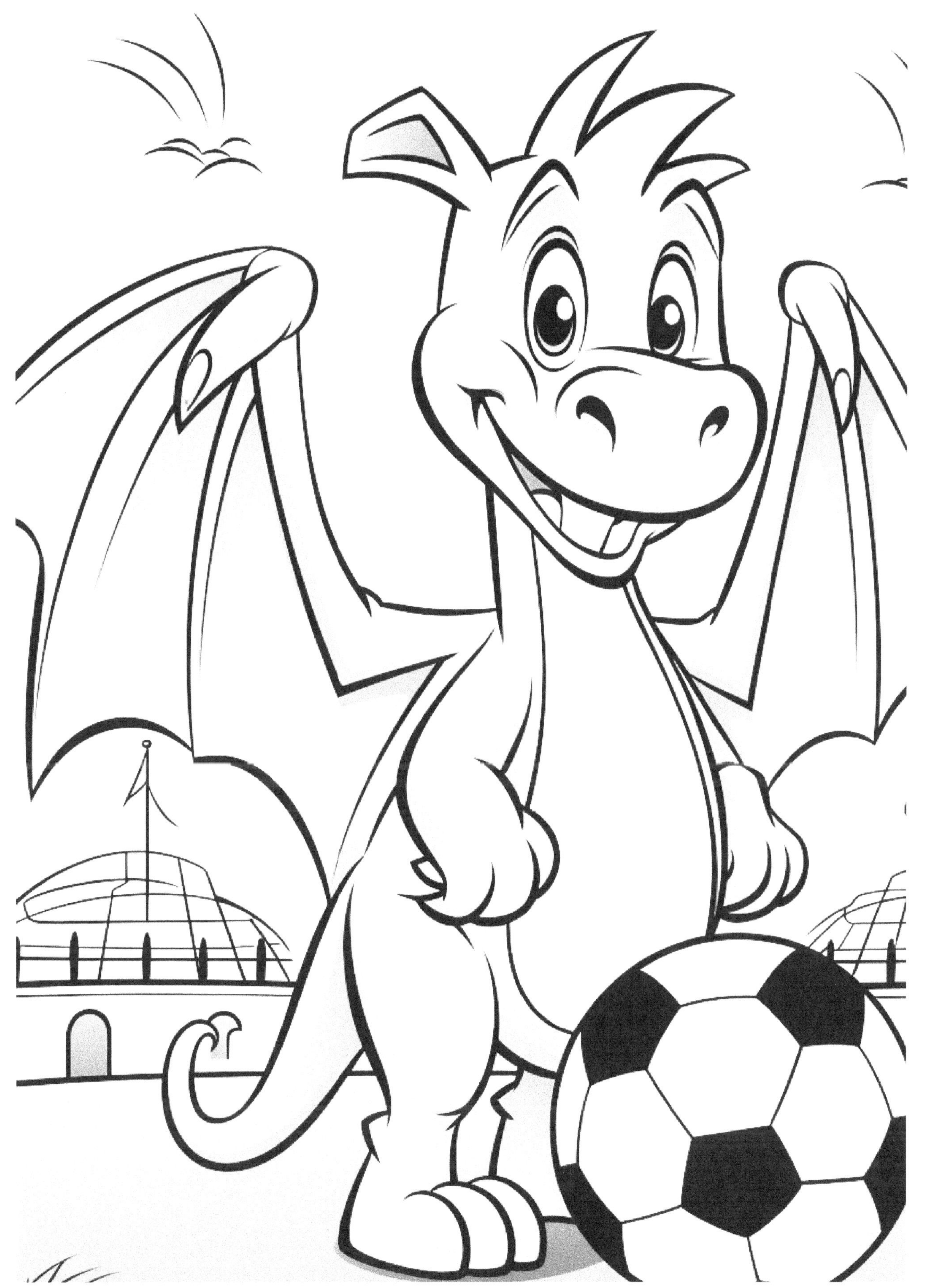

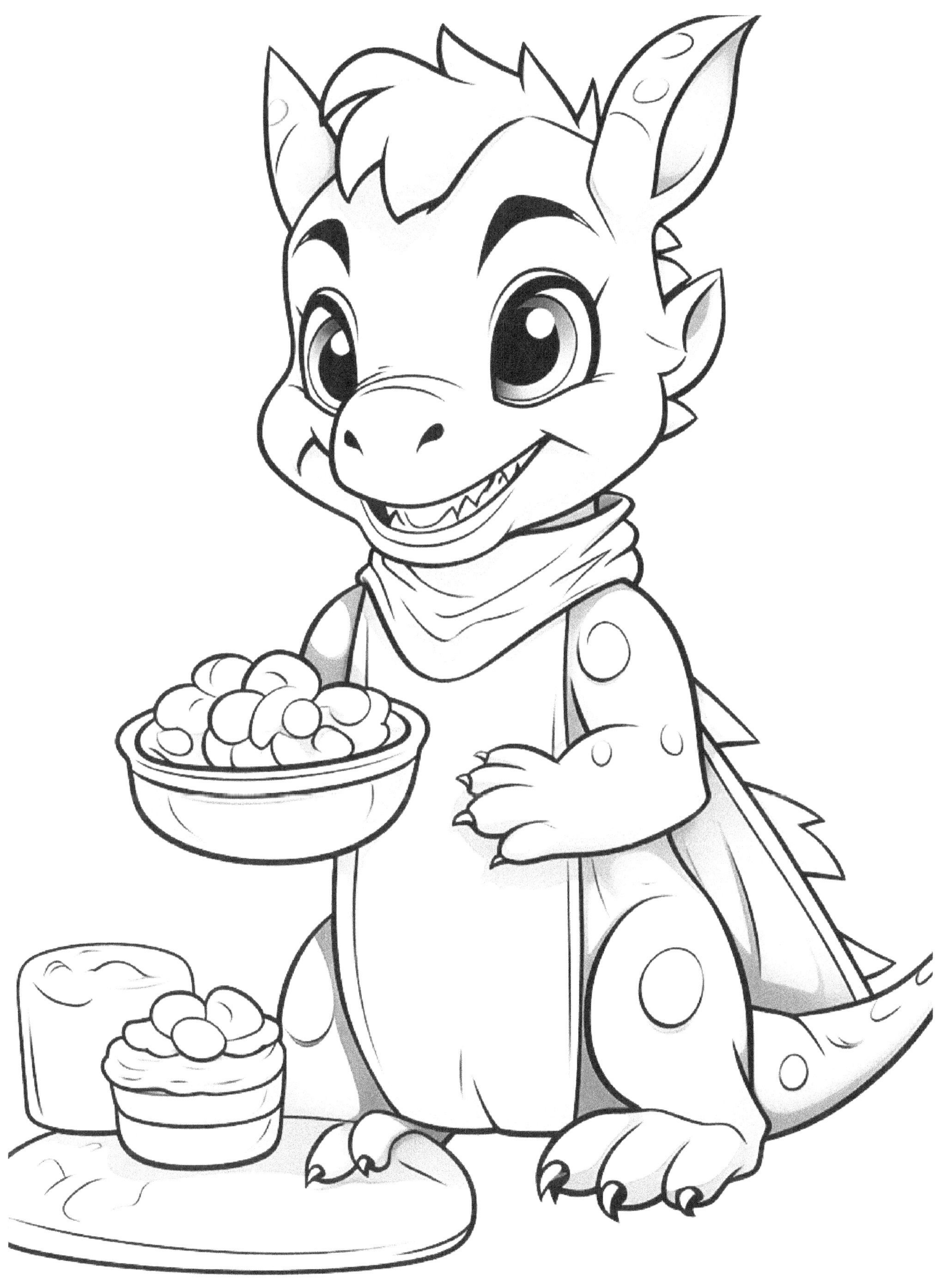

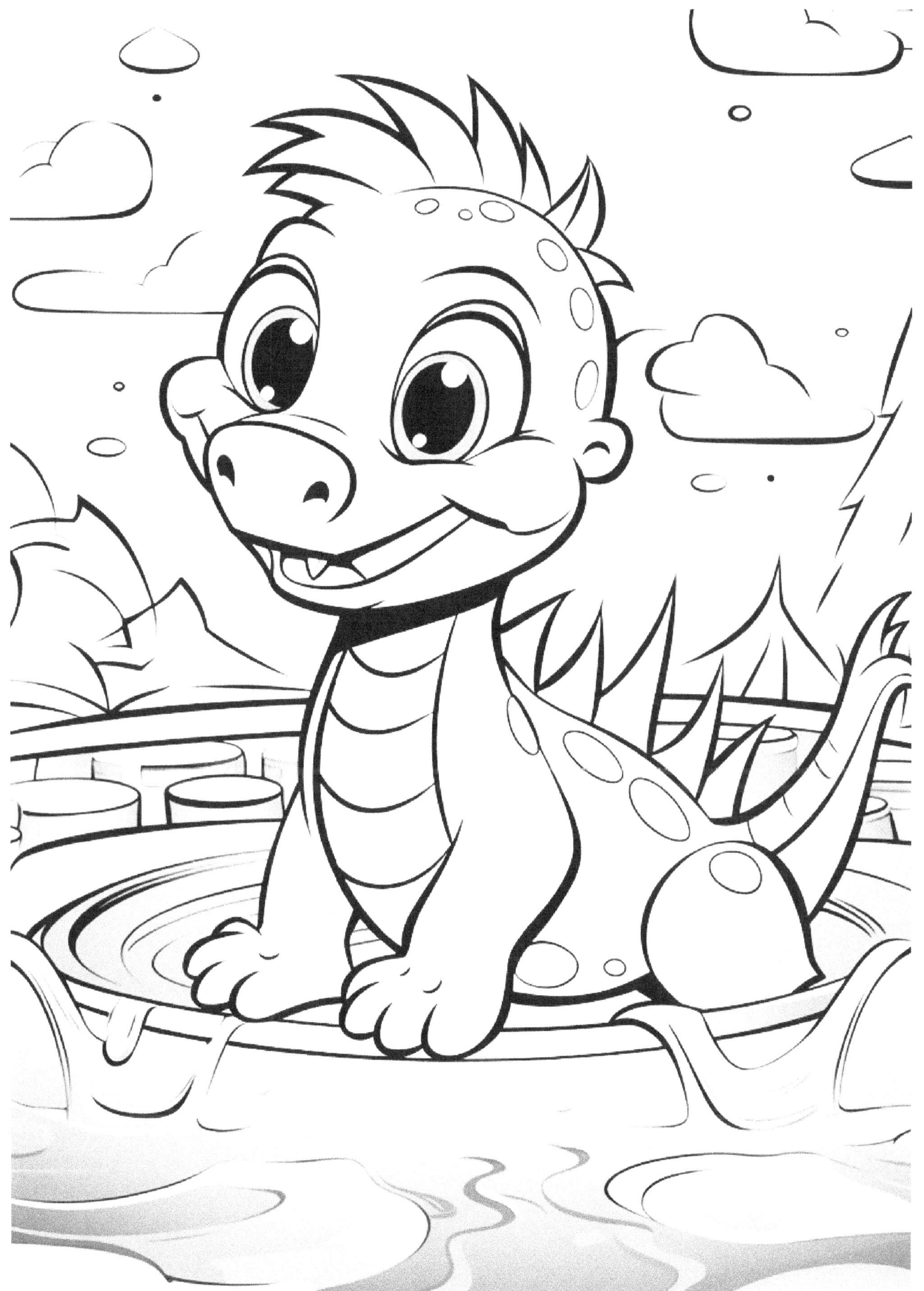

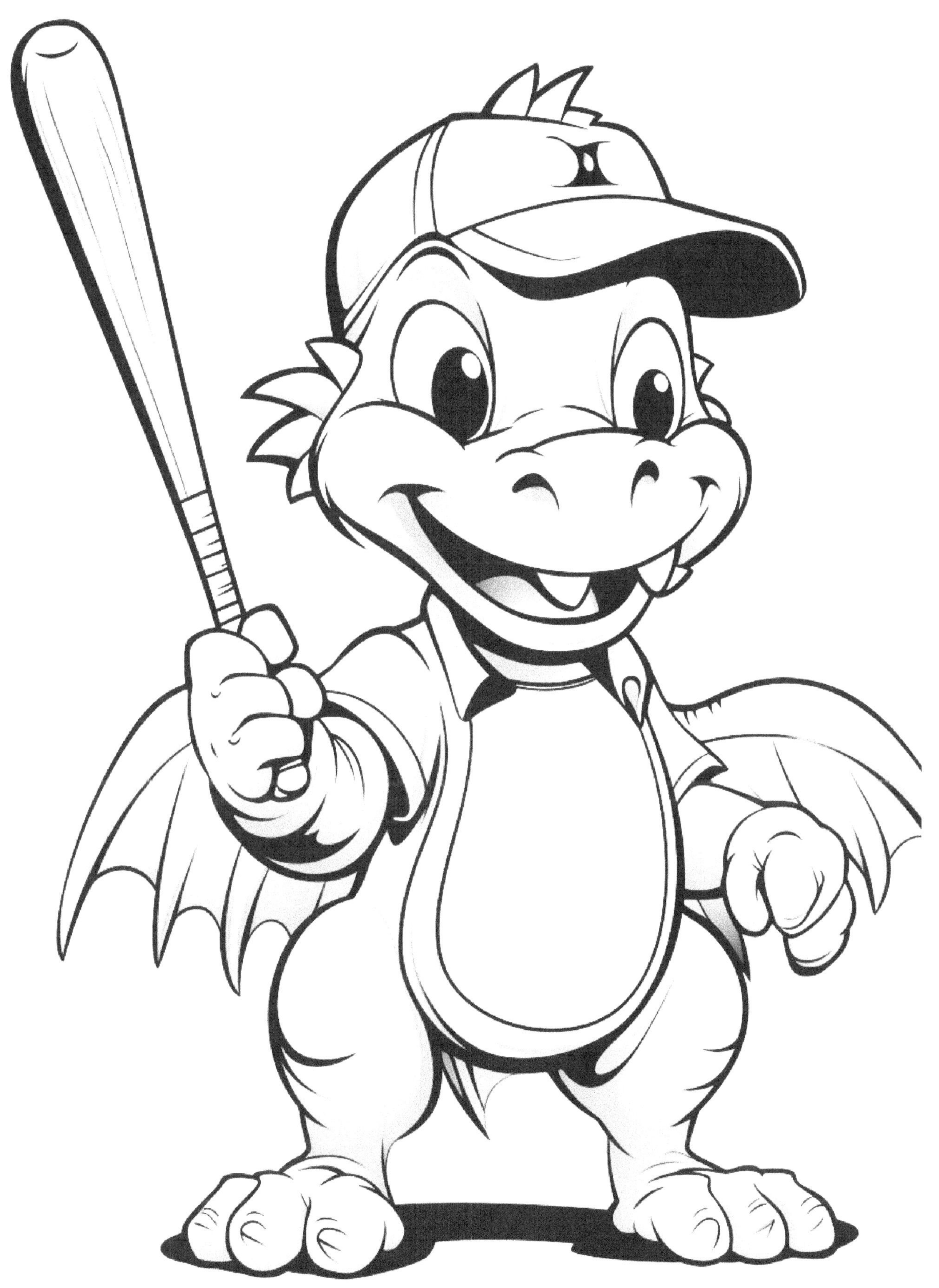

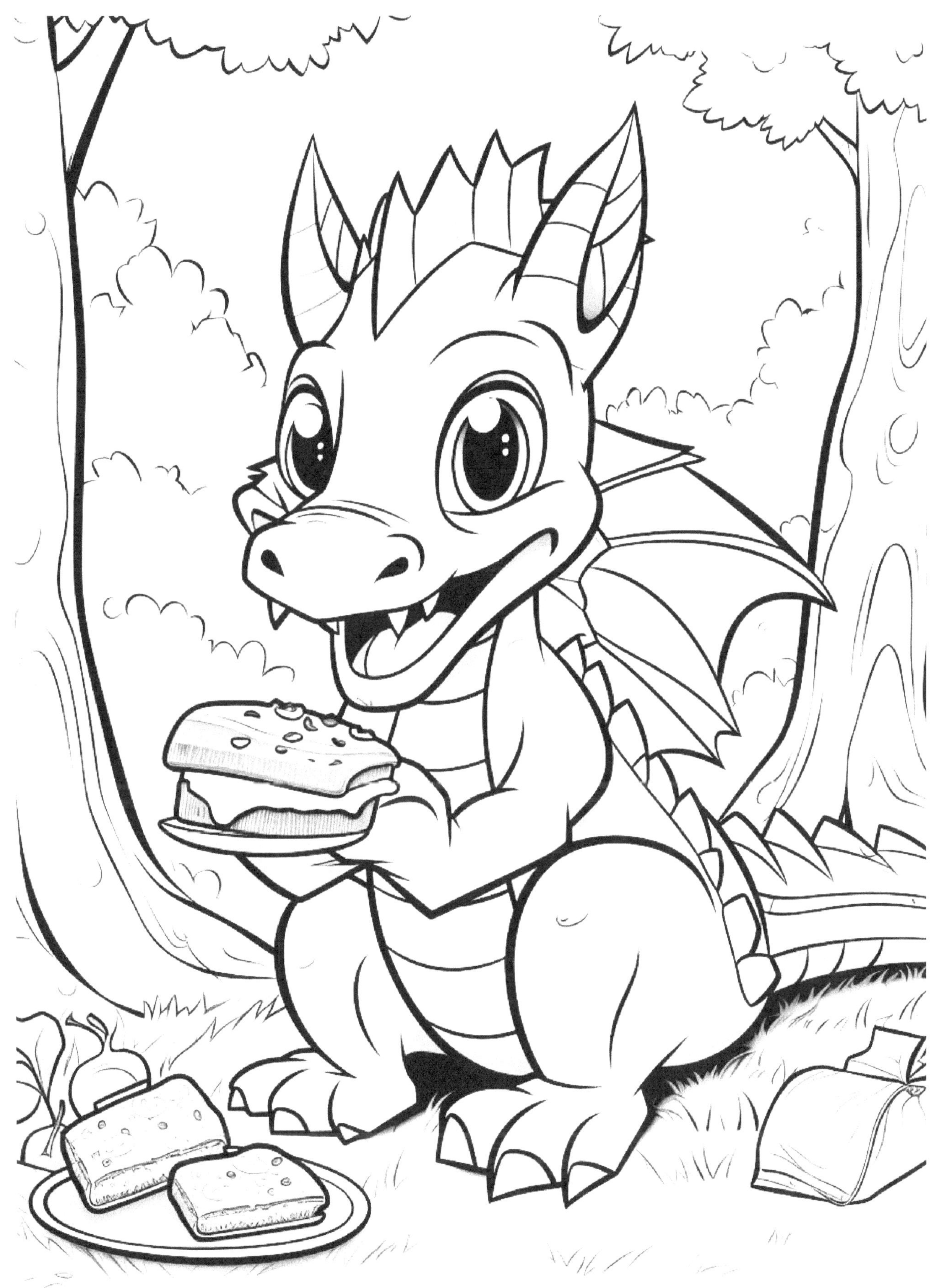

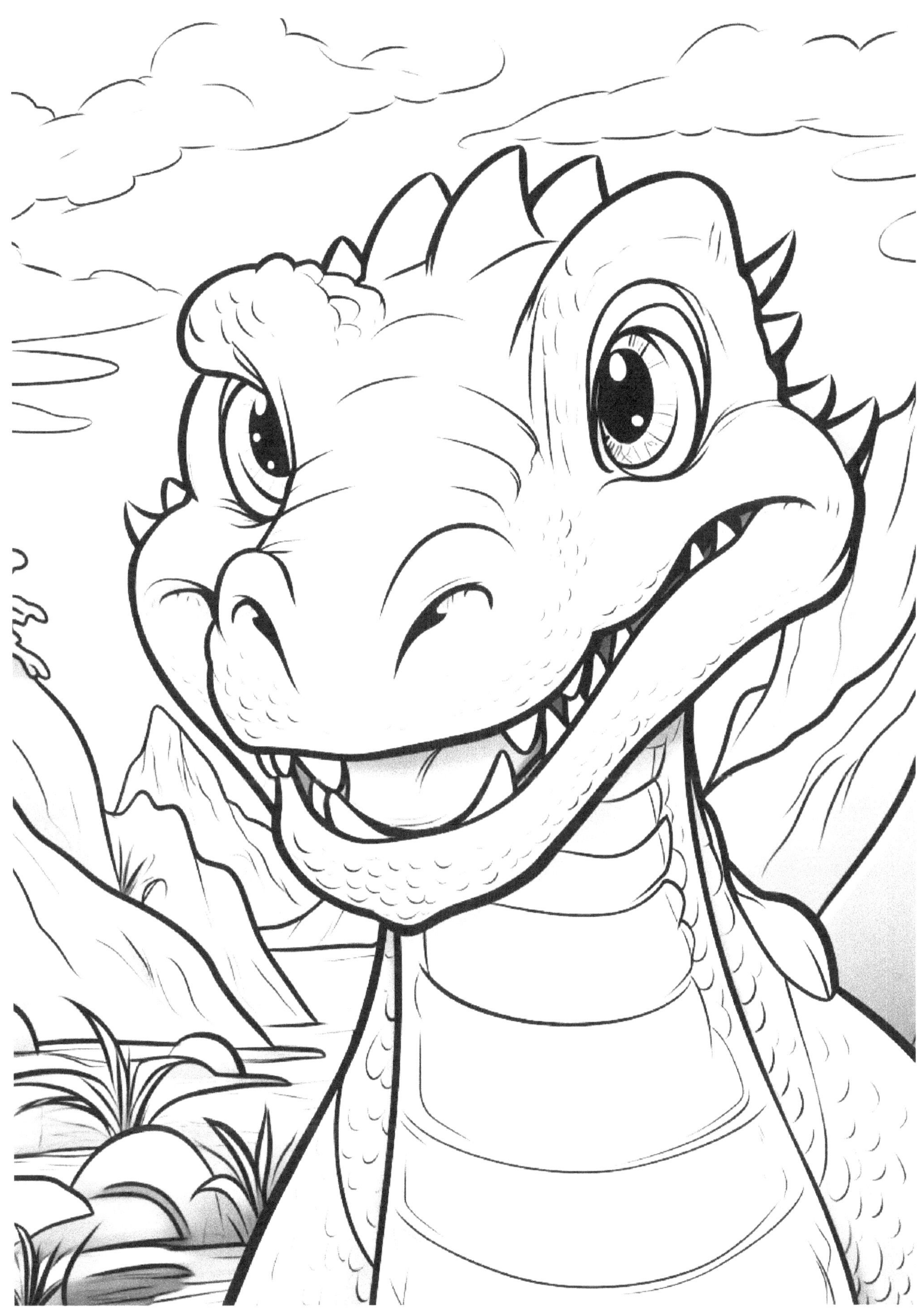

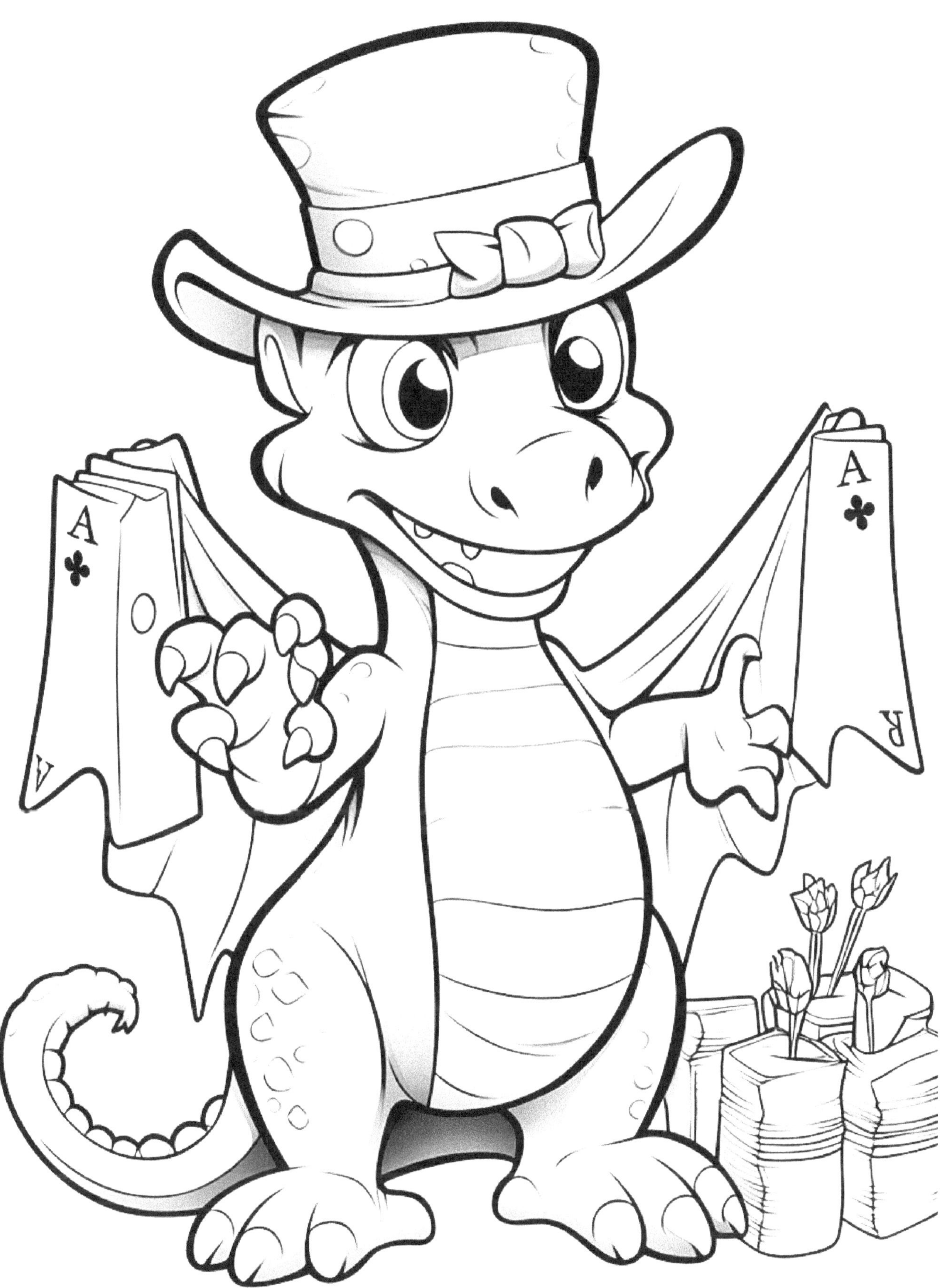
A
♣
A
♣

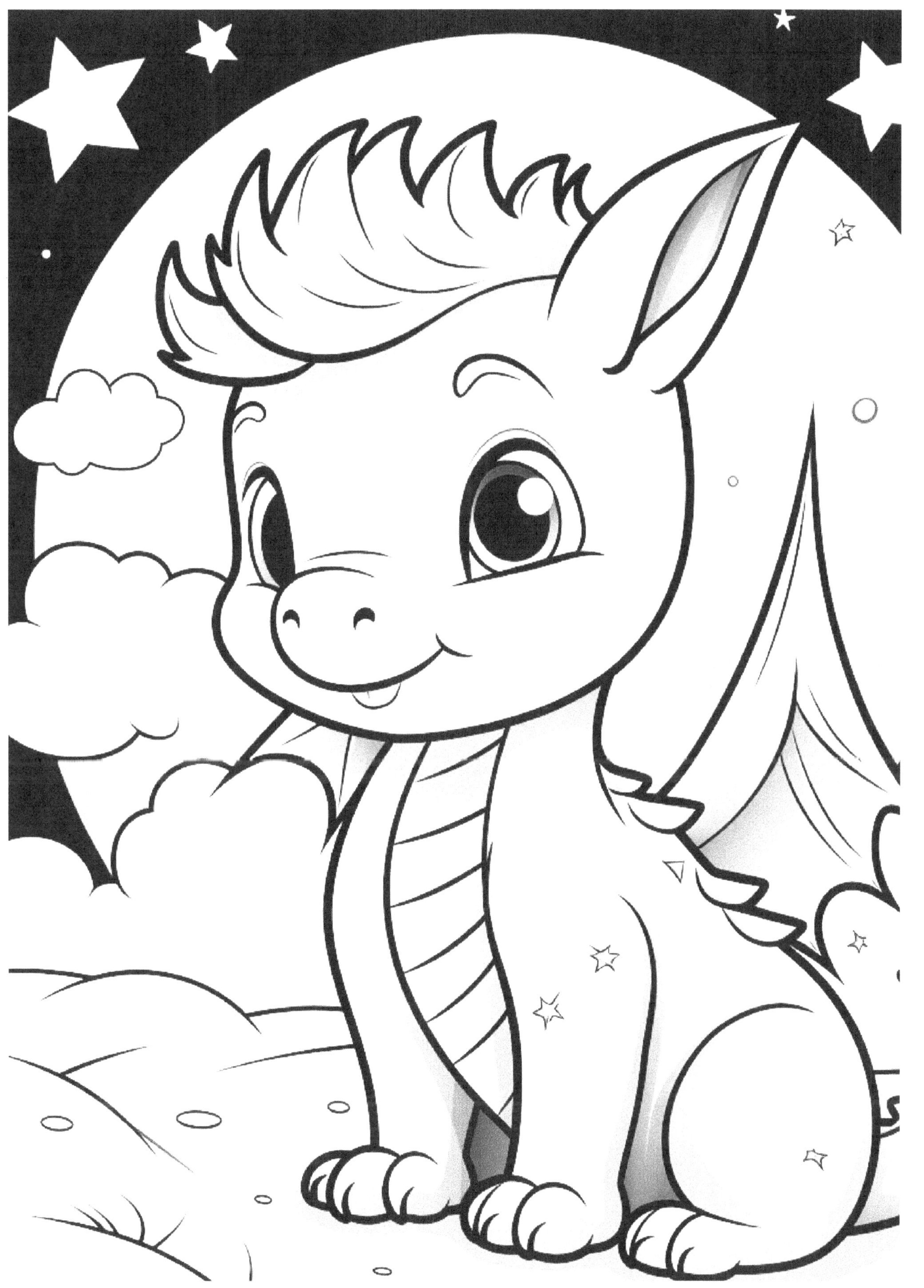

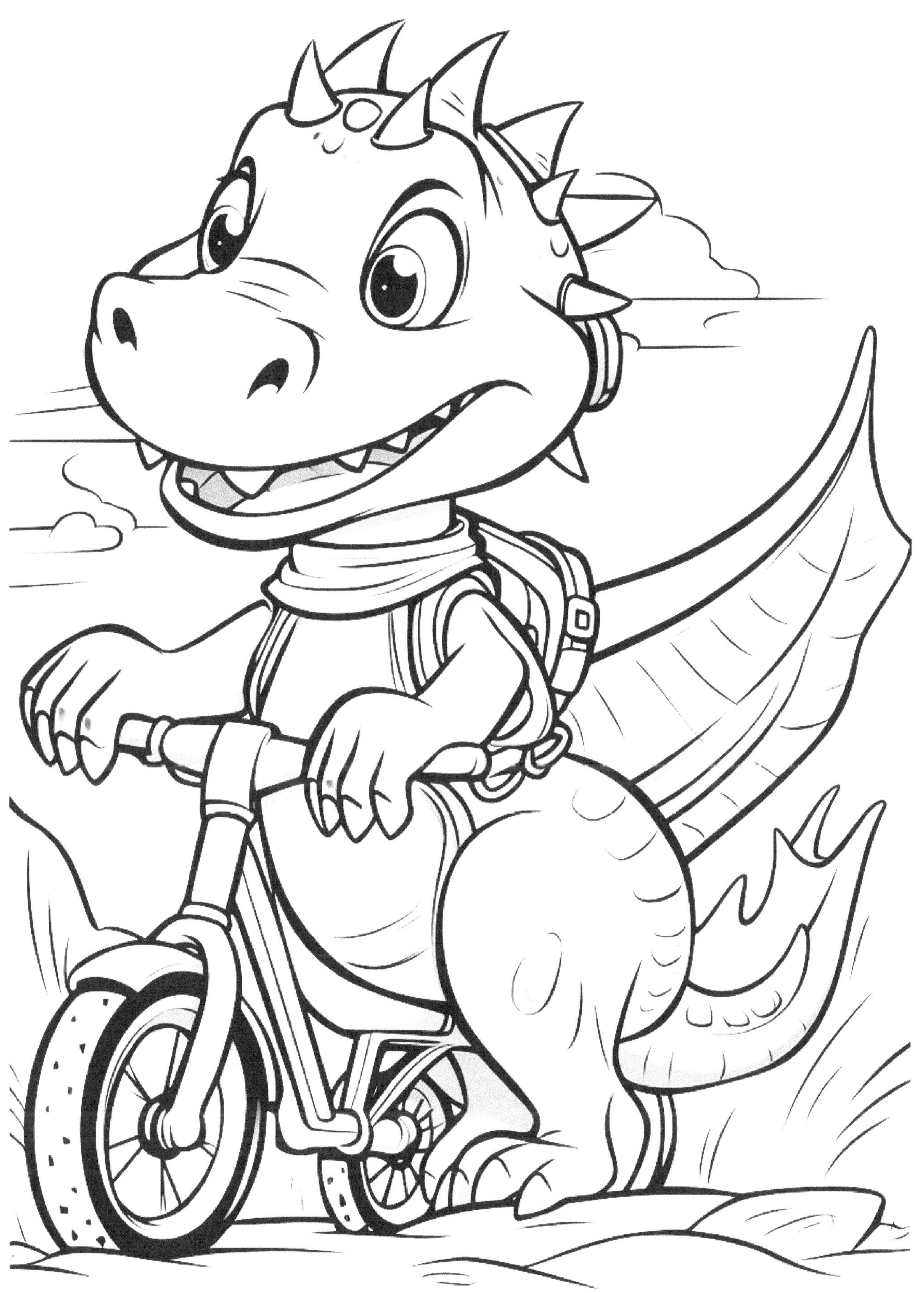

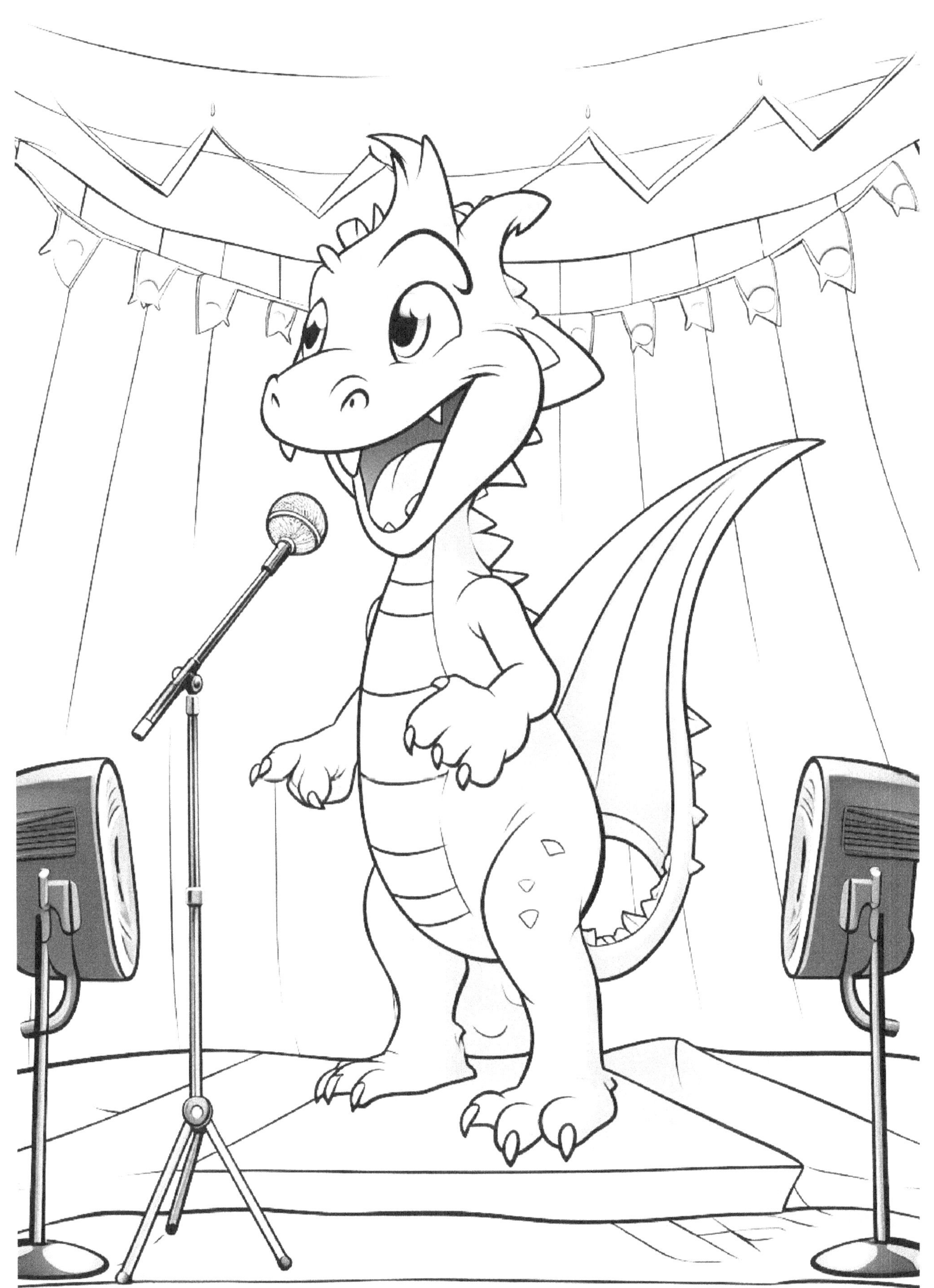

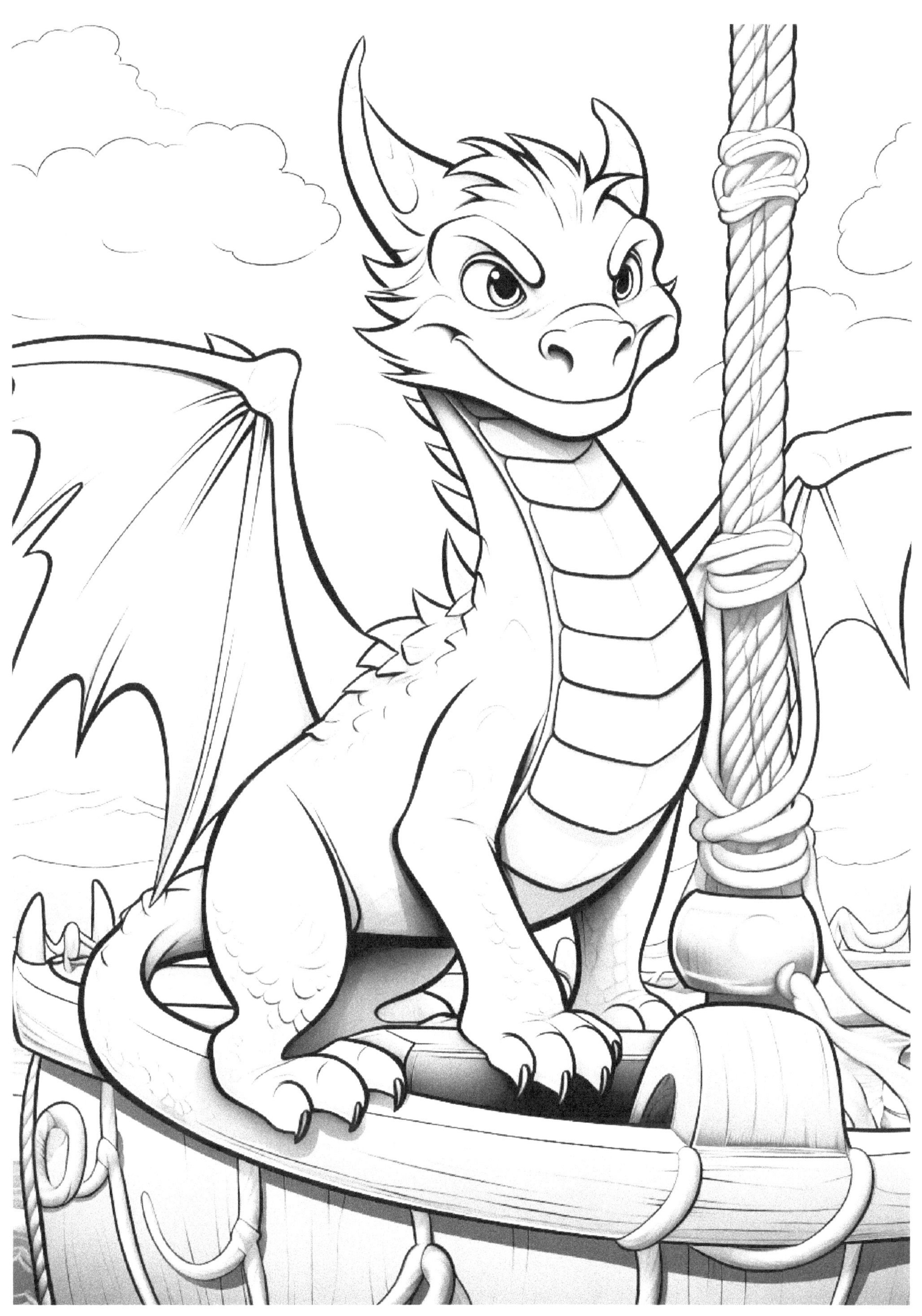

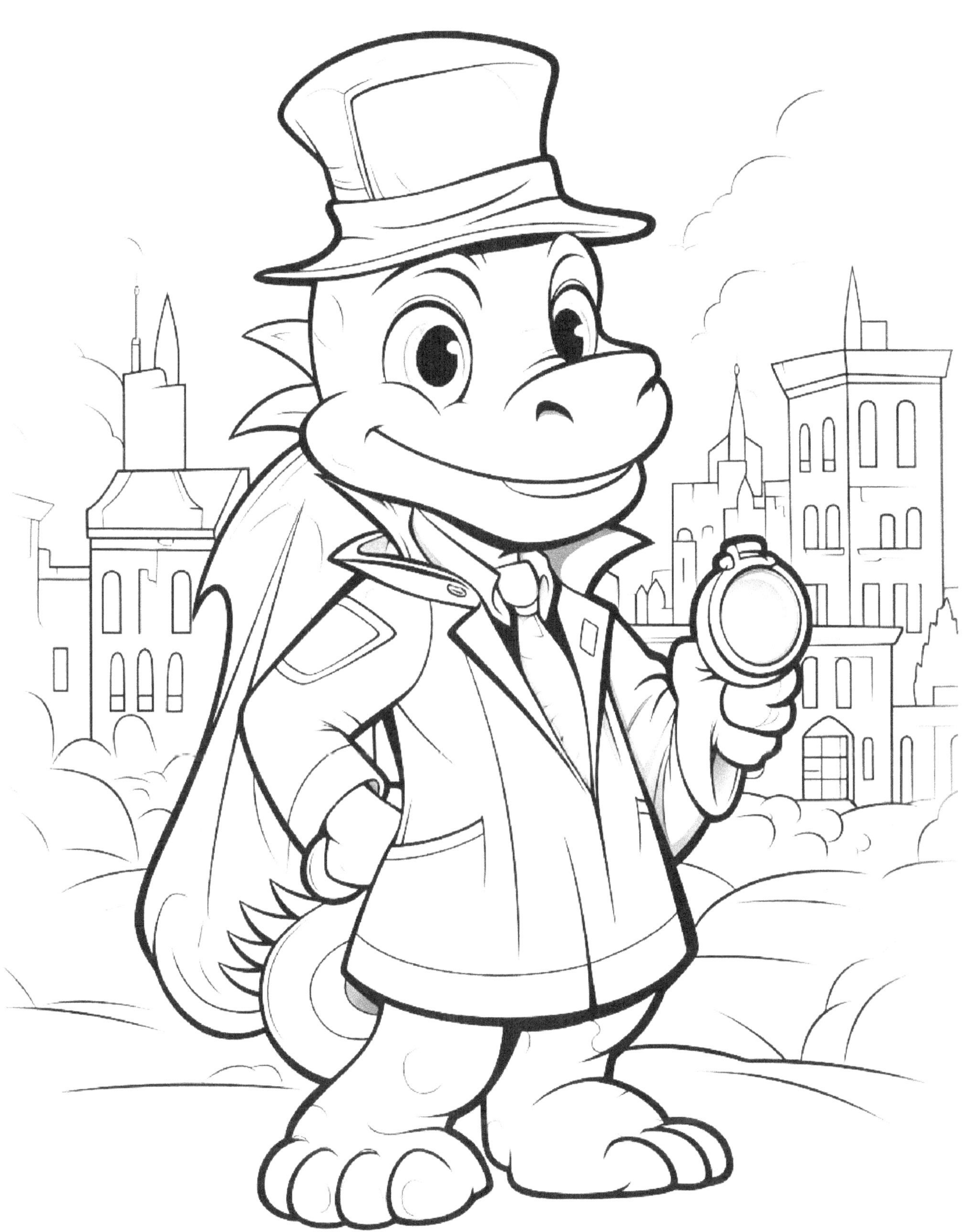

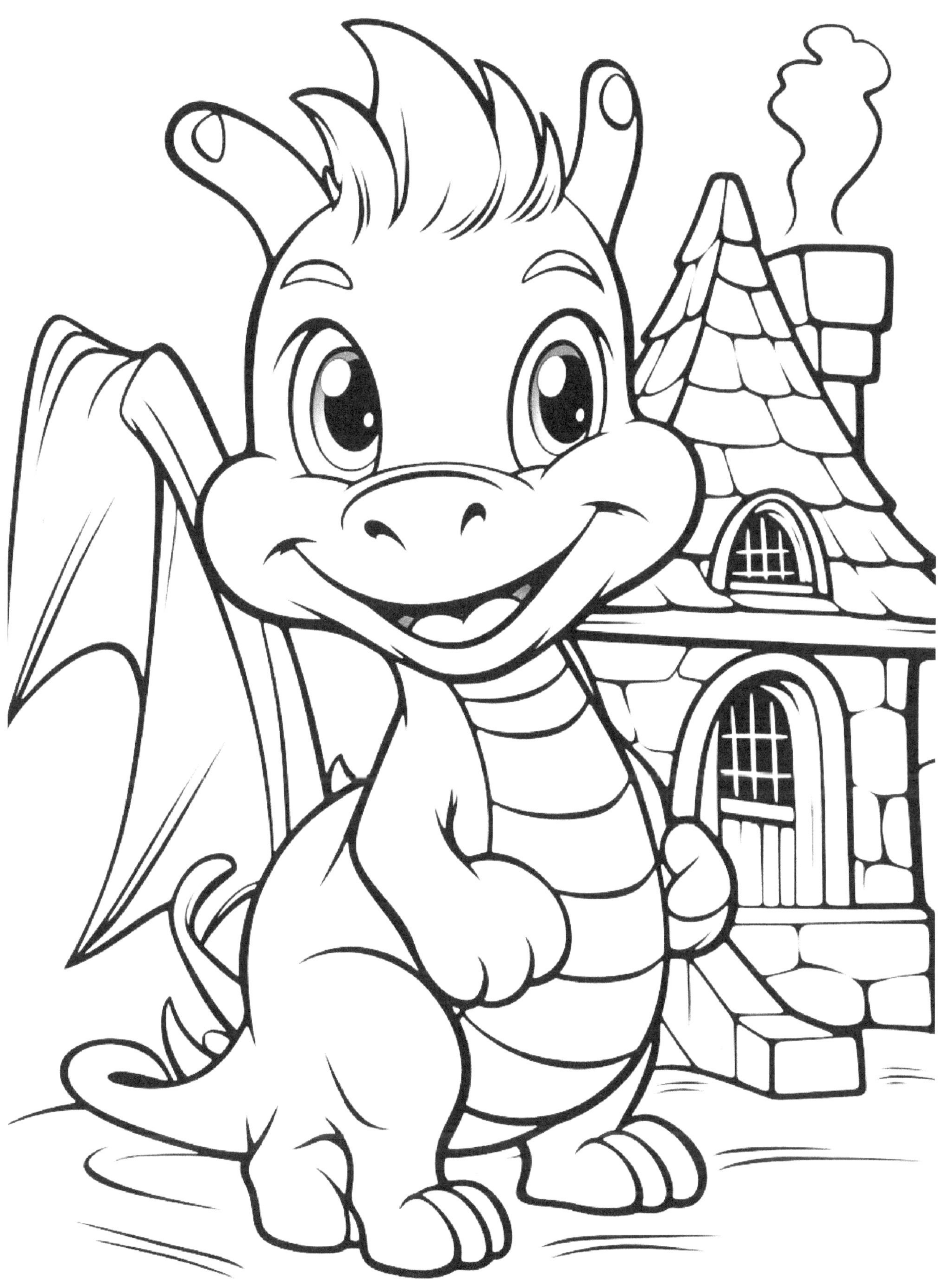

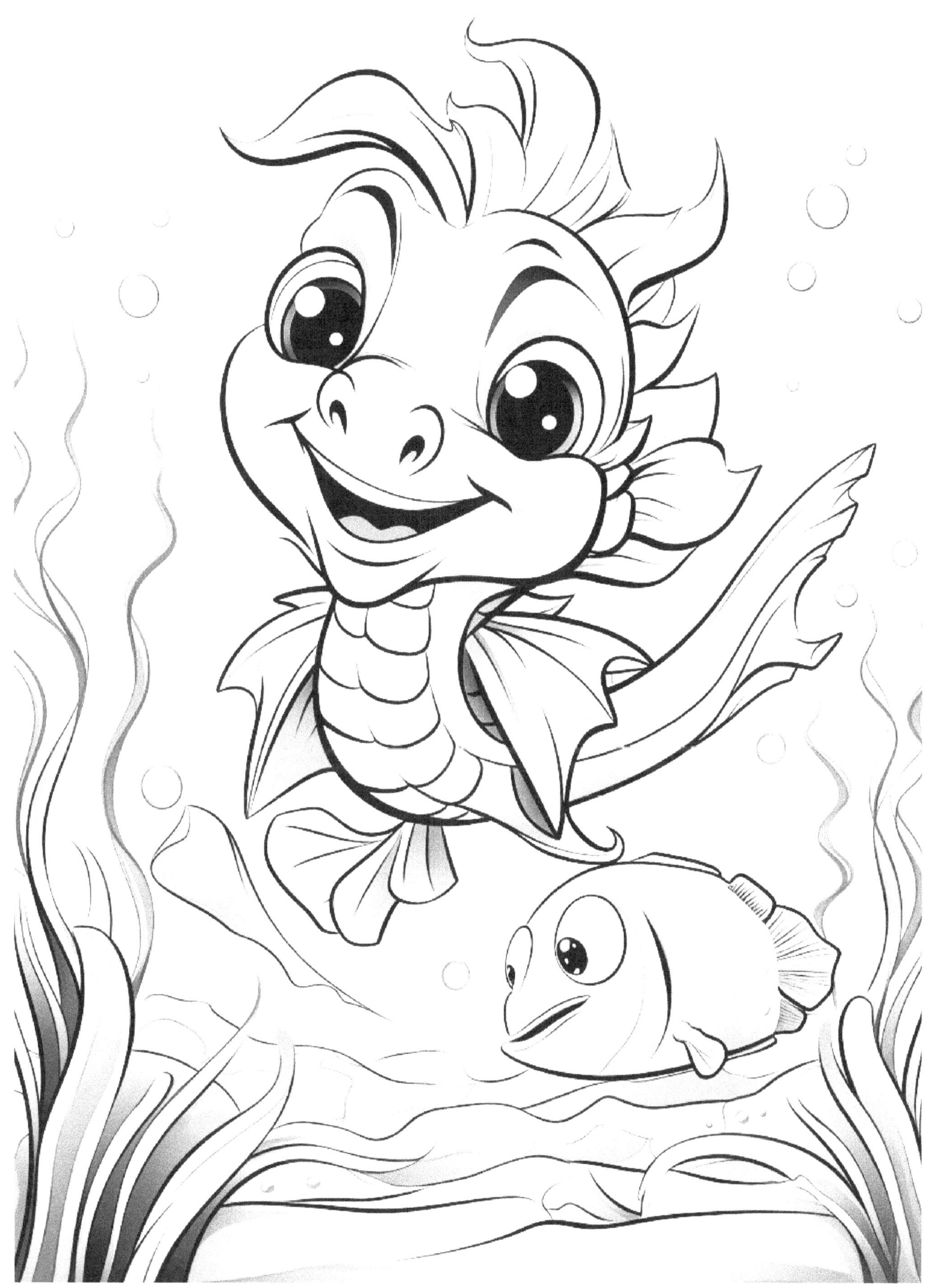

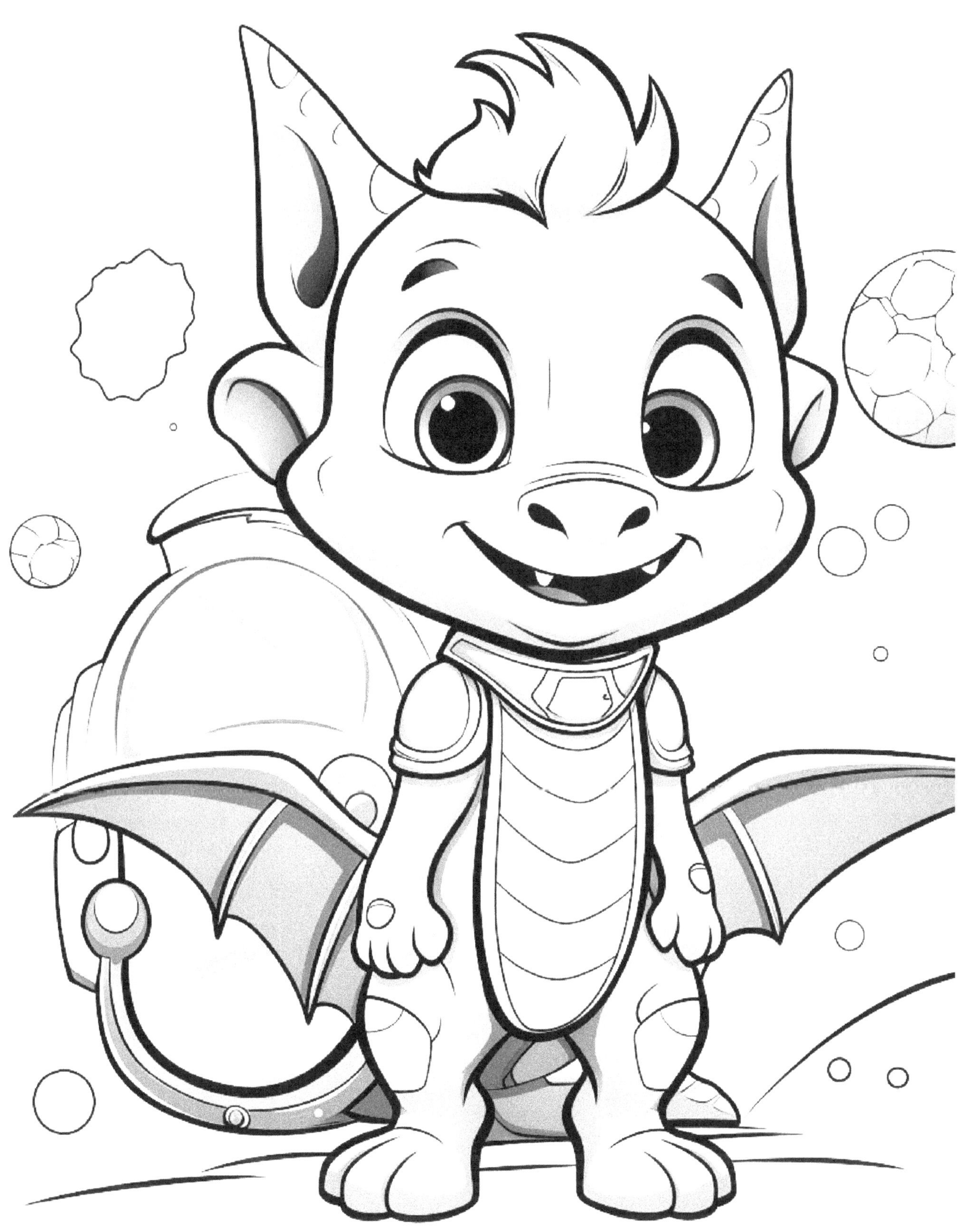

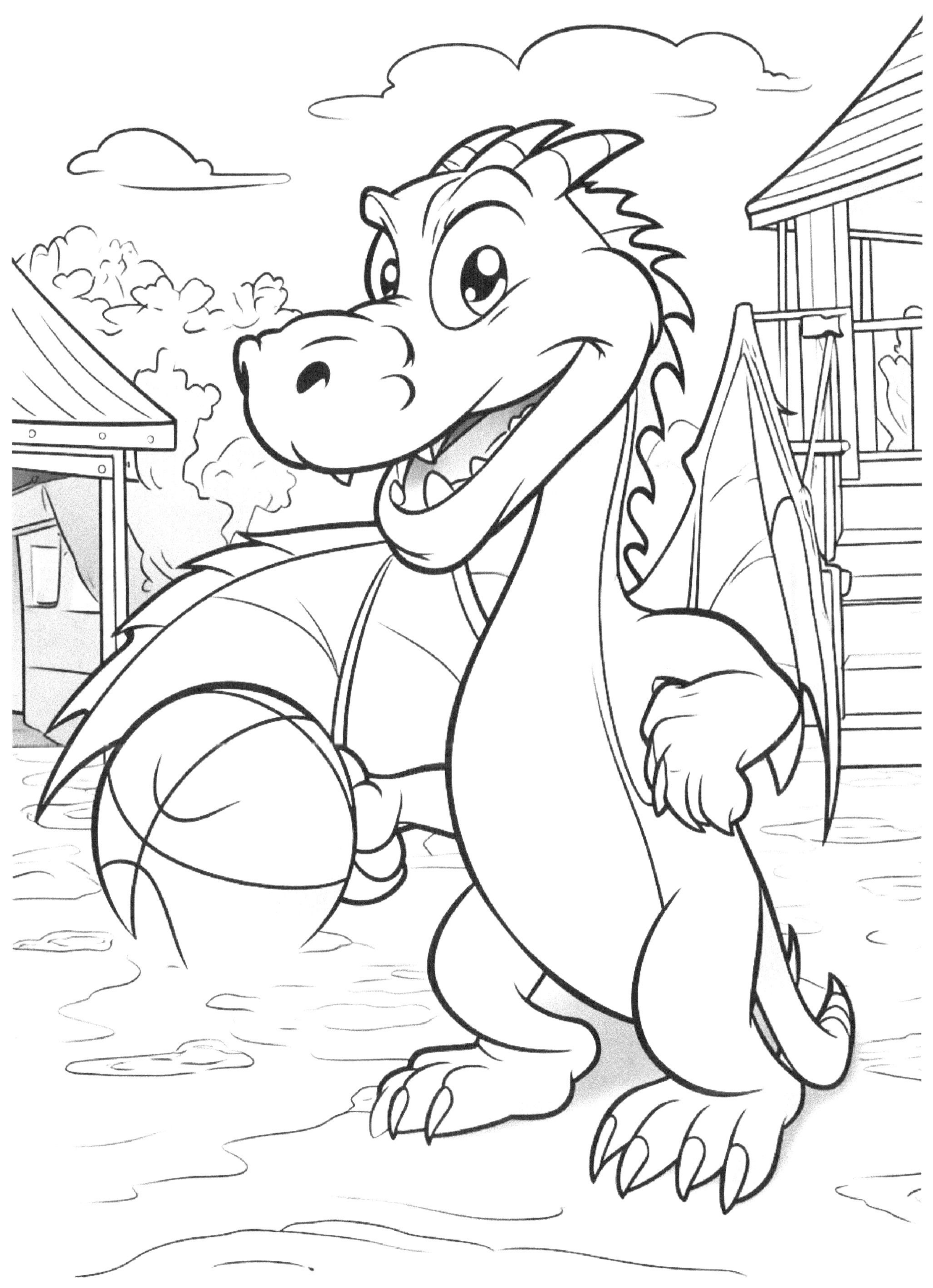

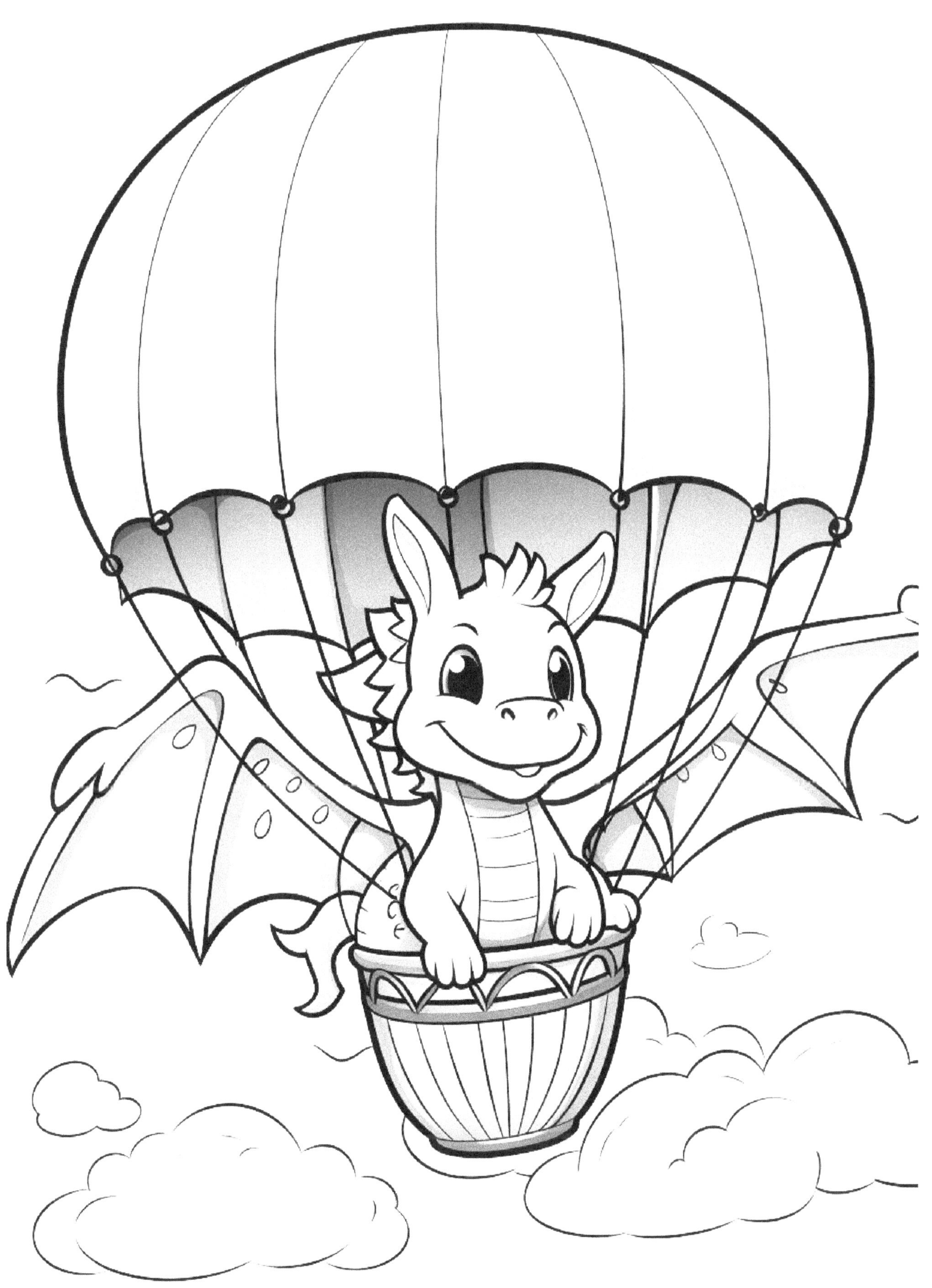

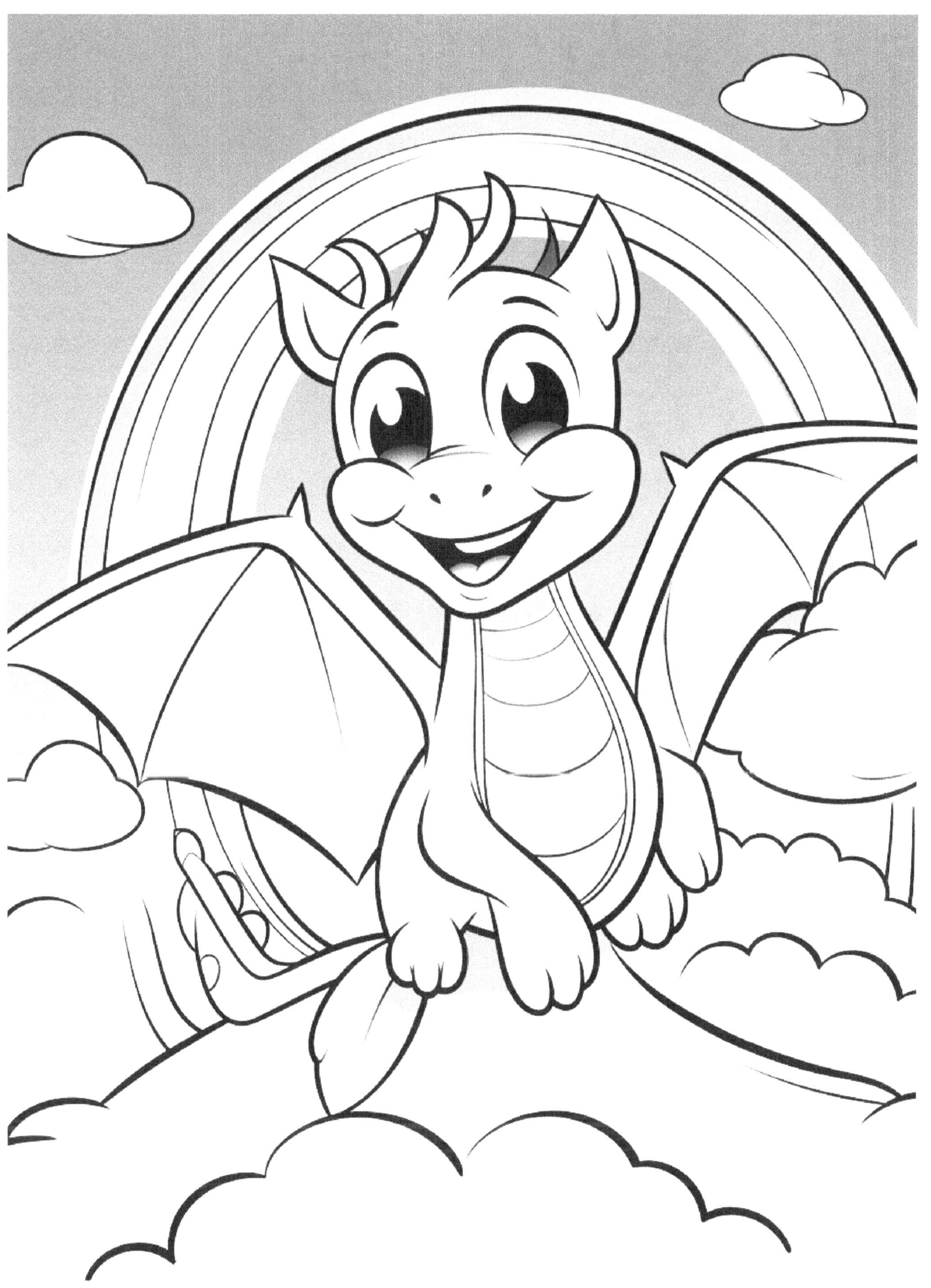

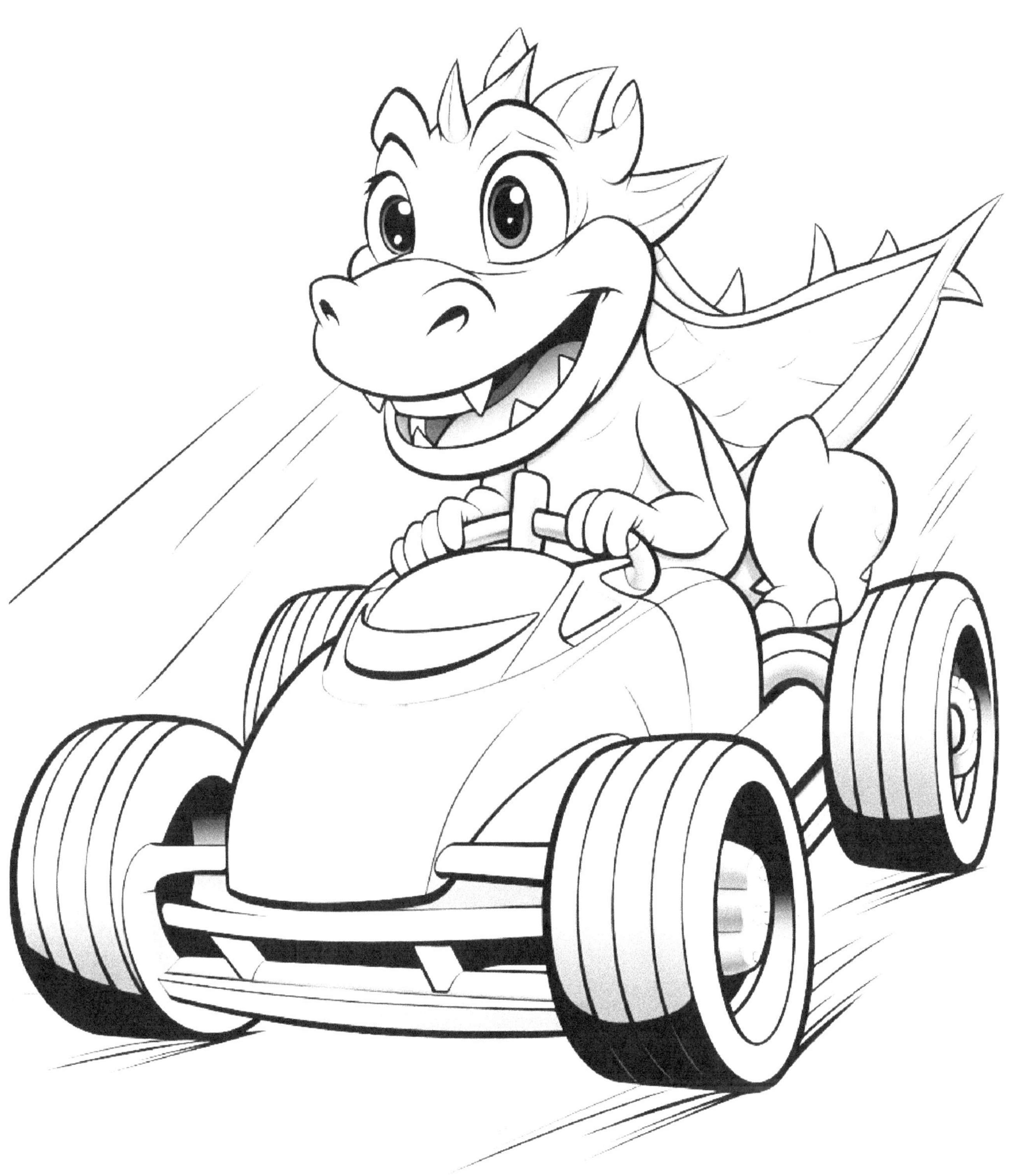

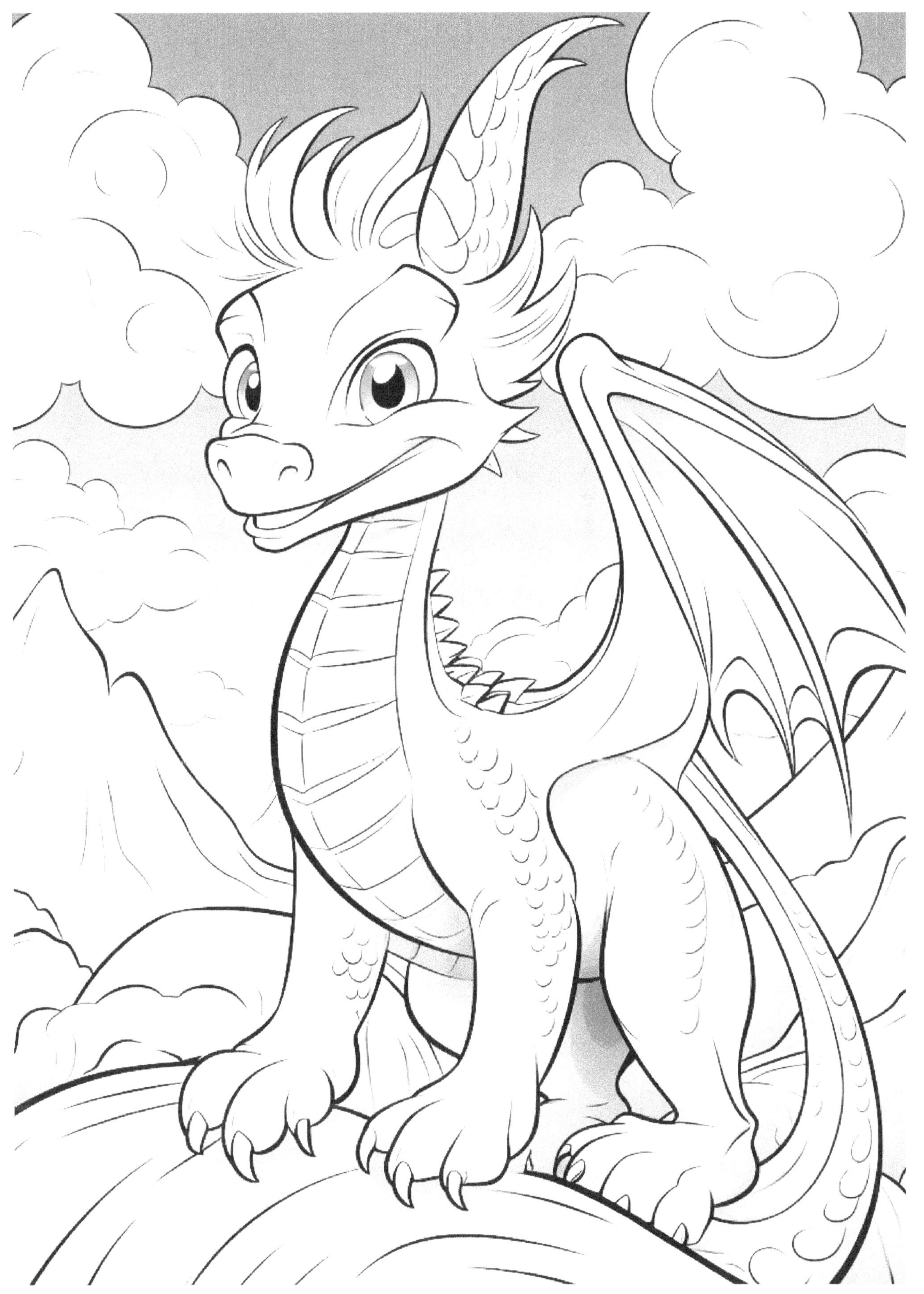

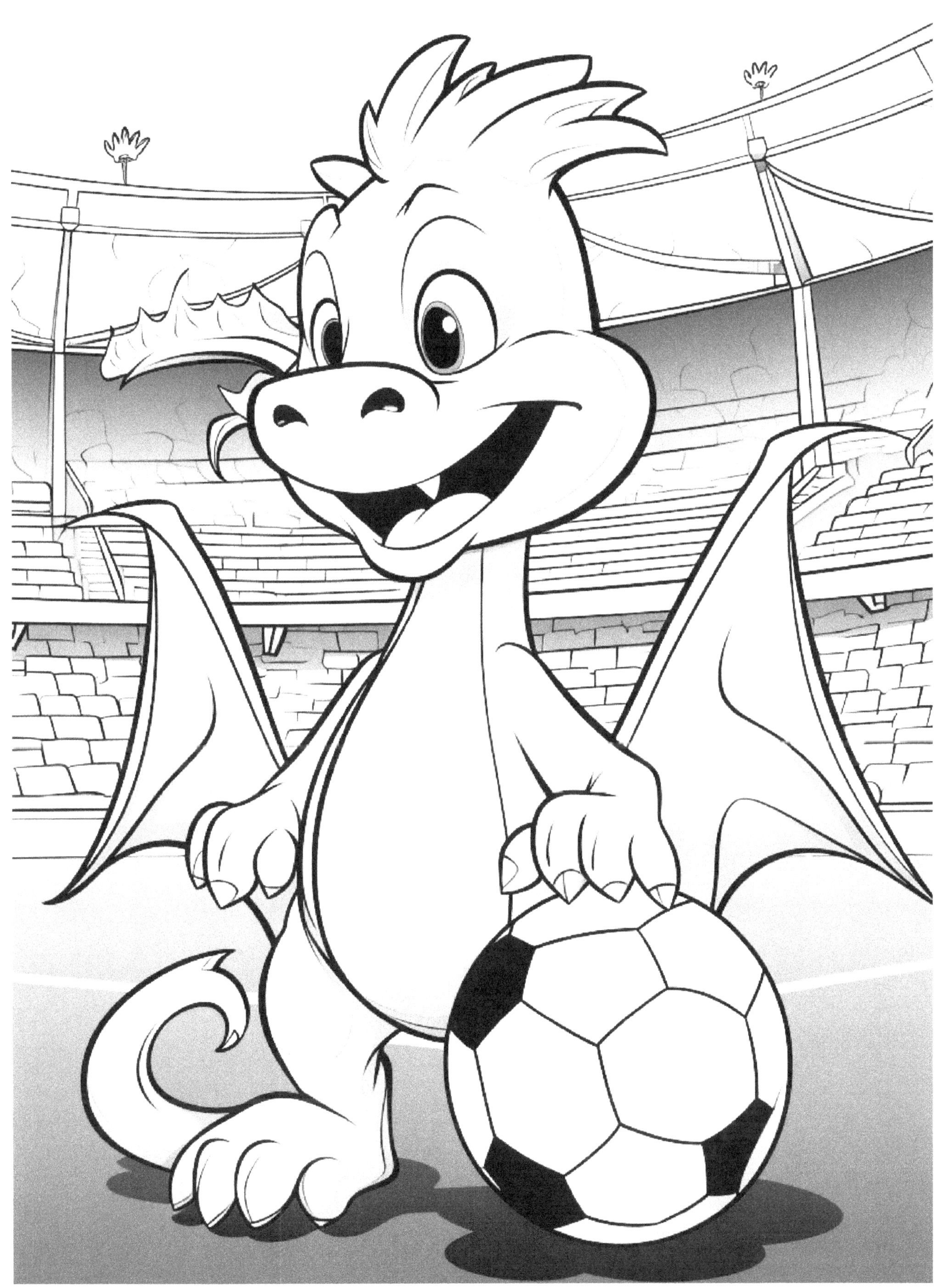

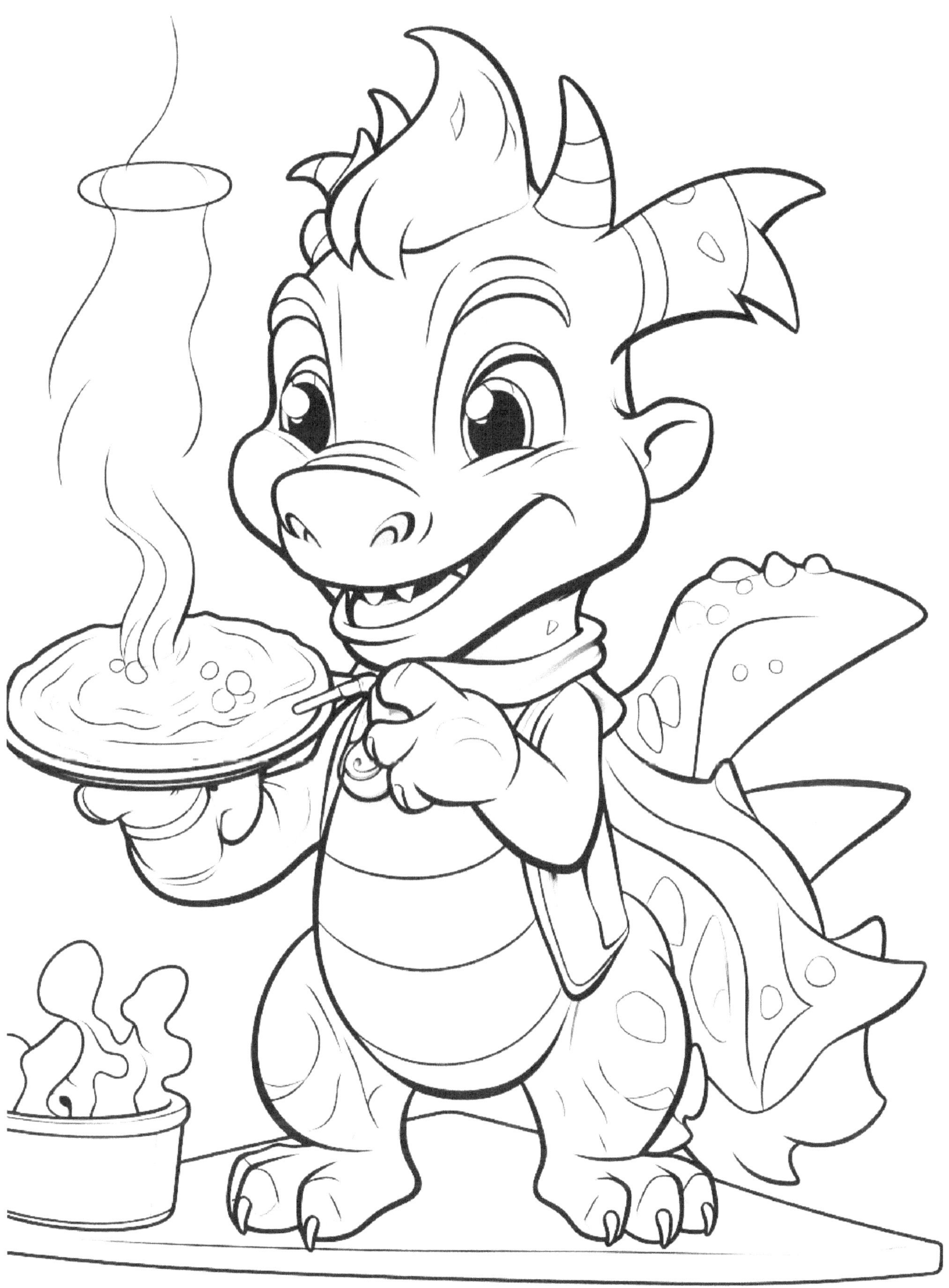

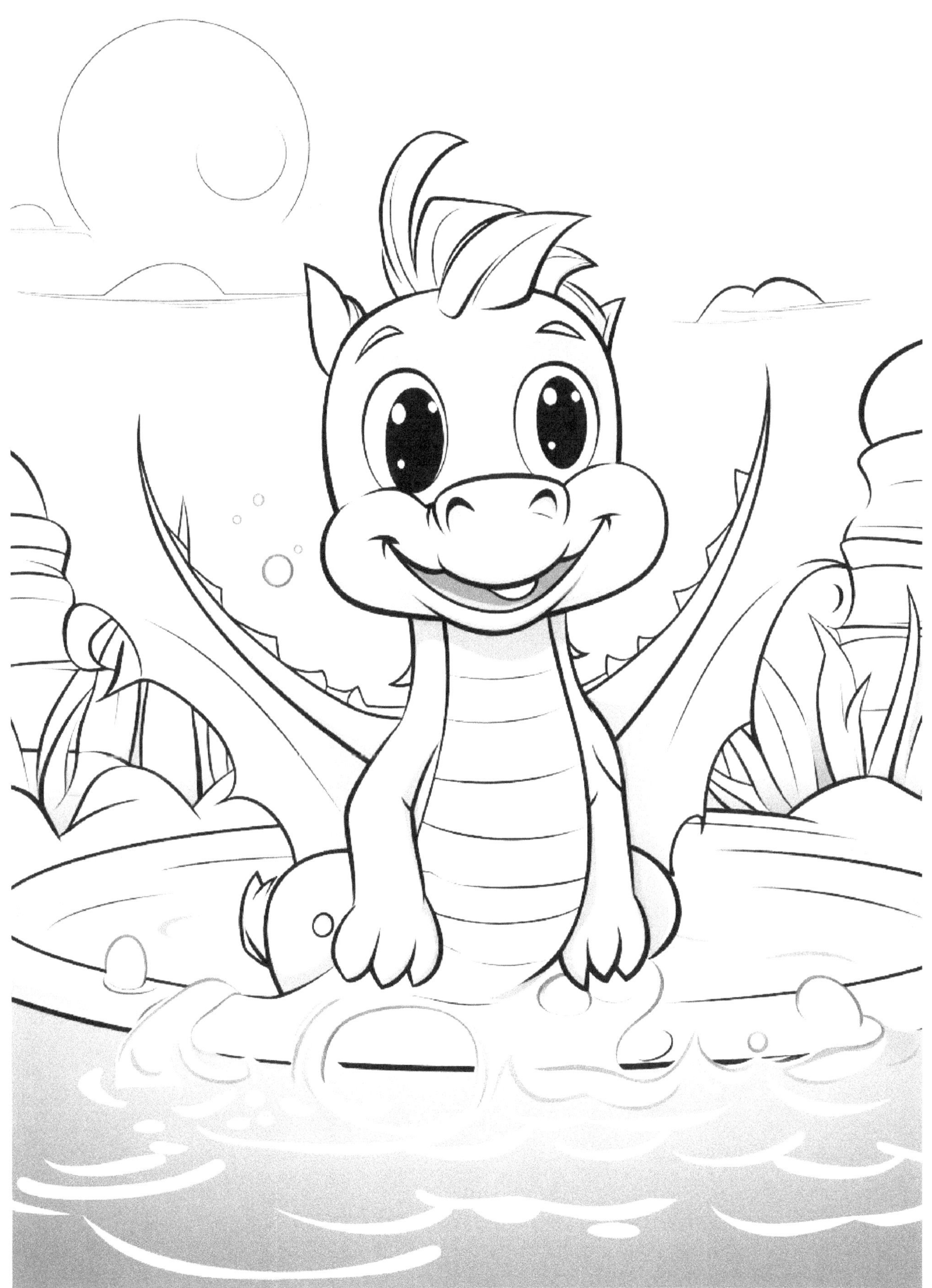

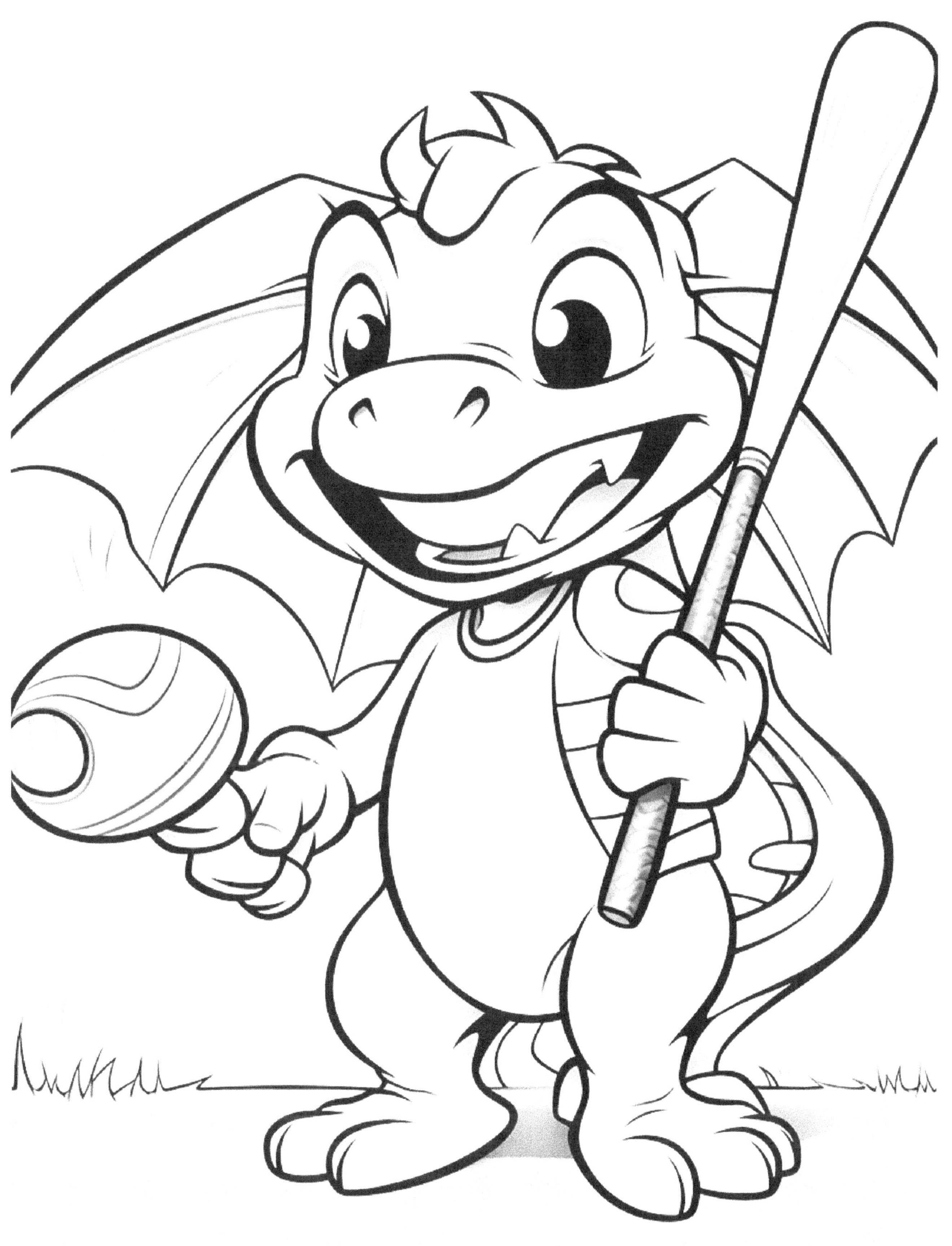

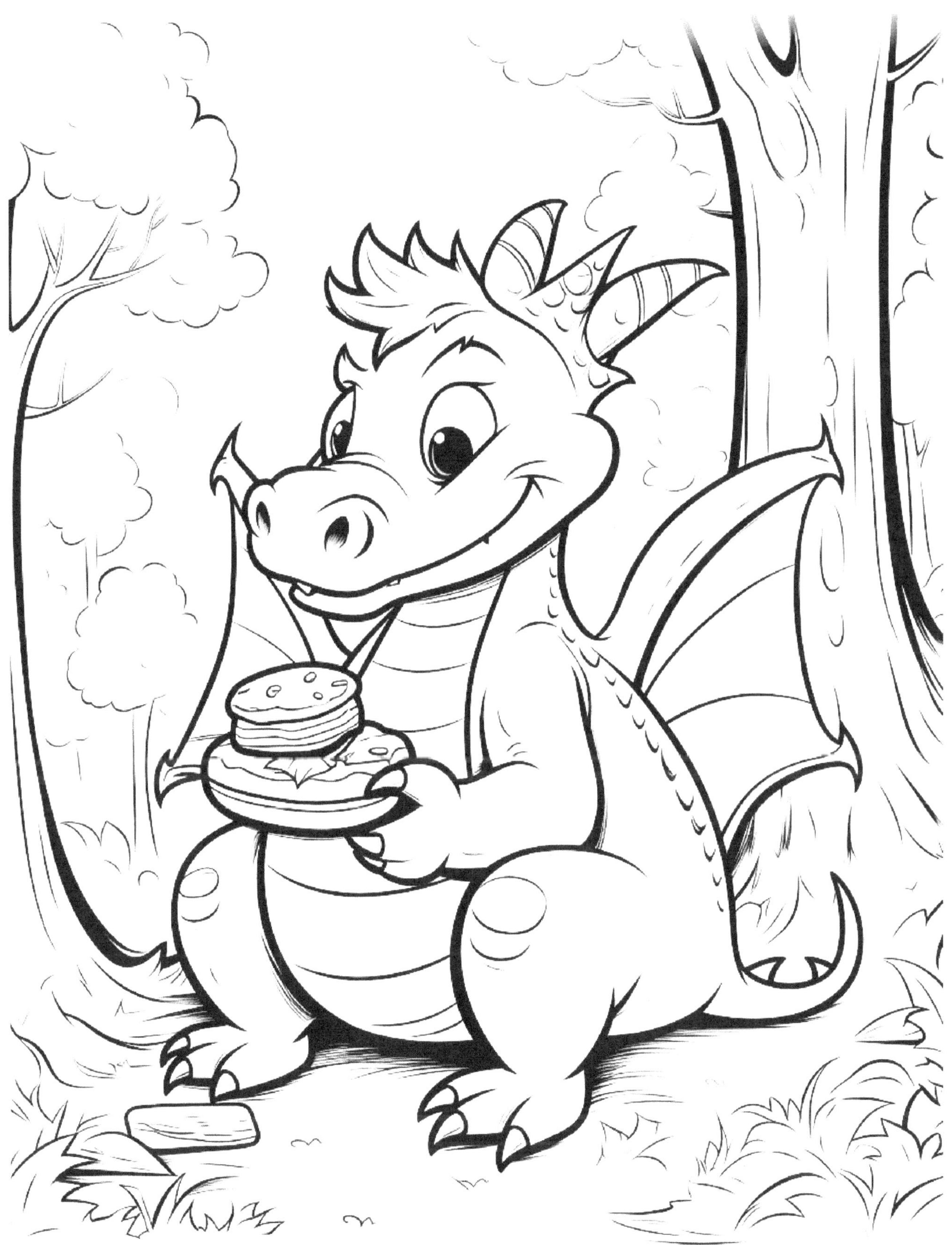

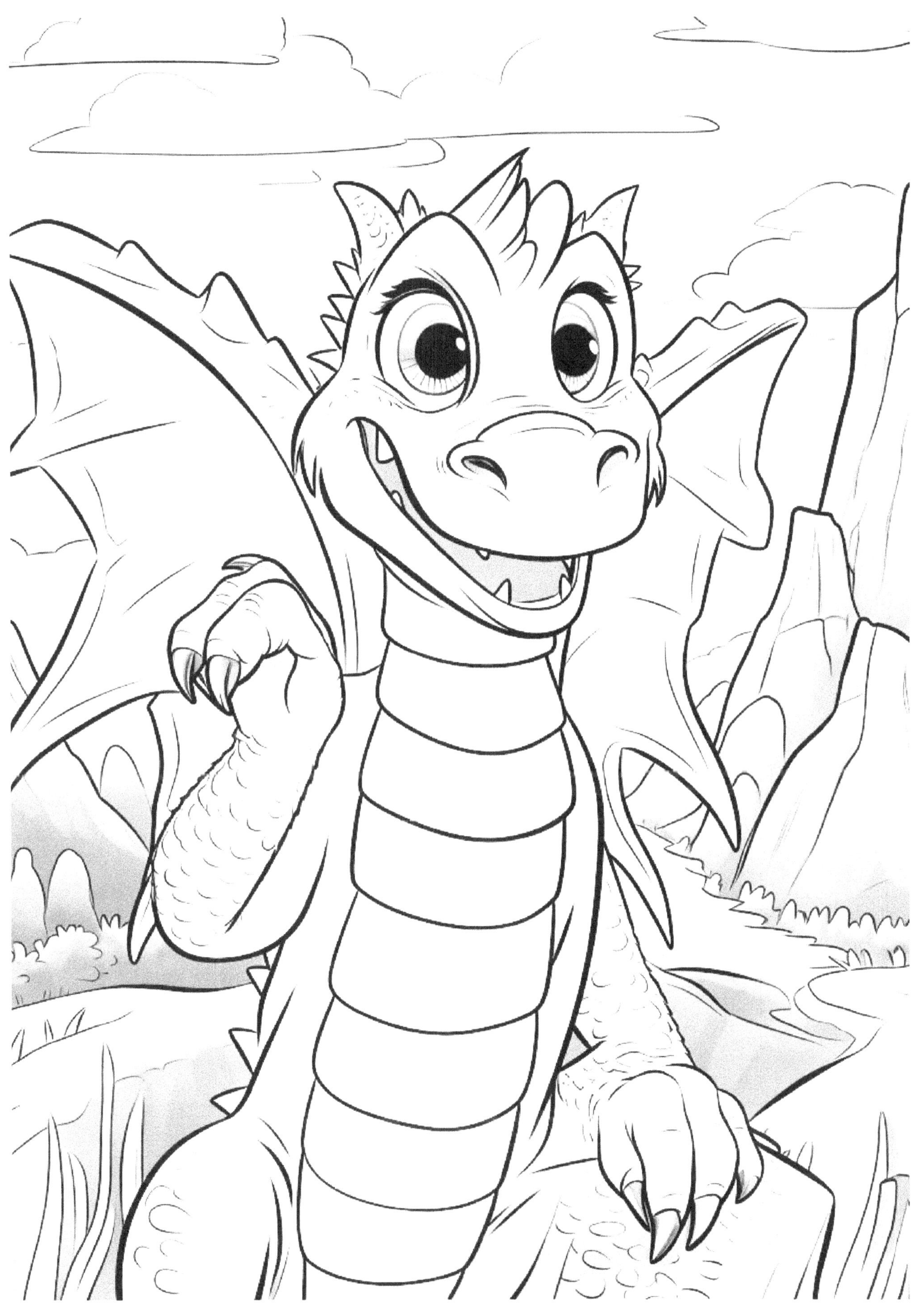

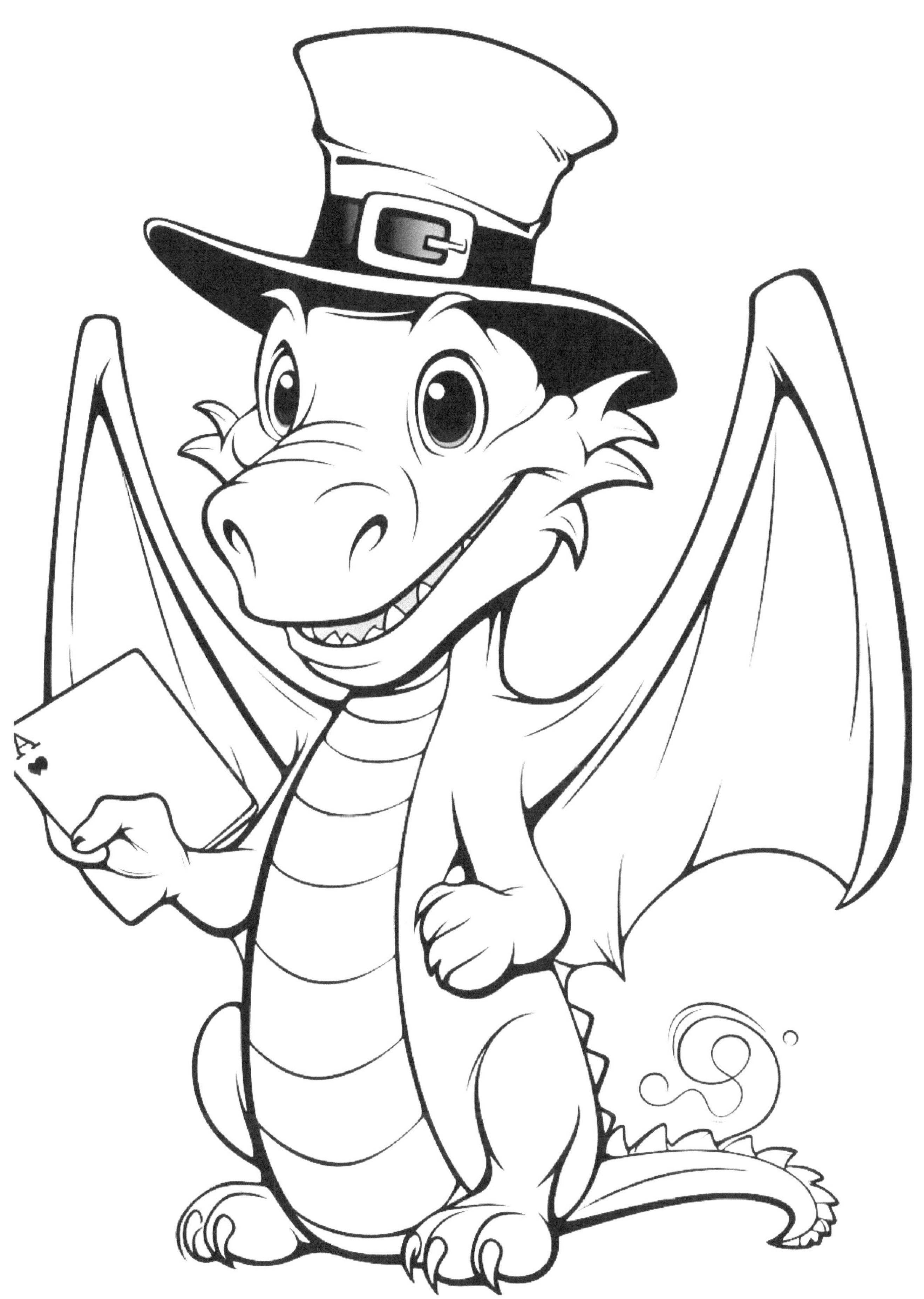

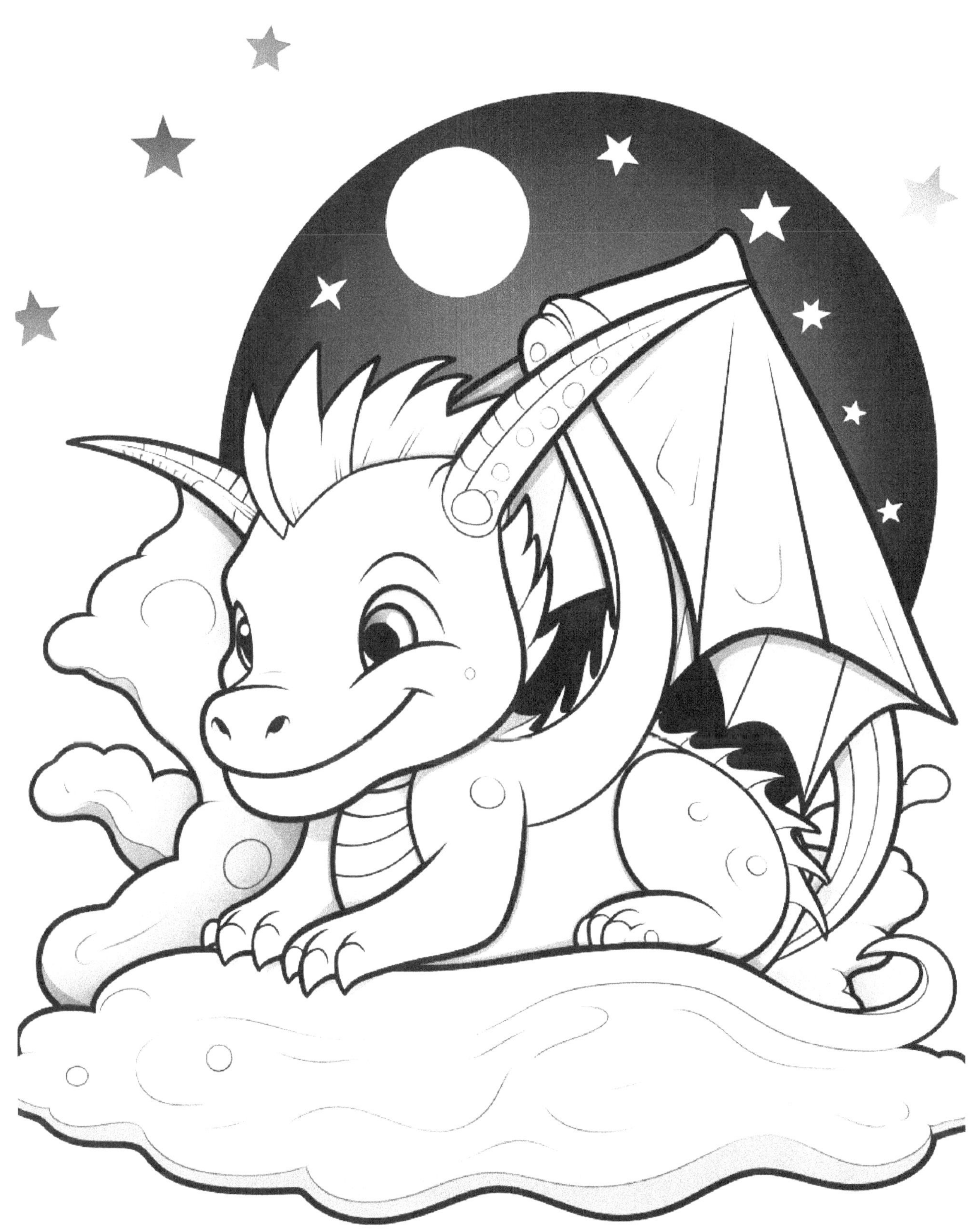

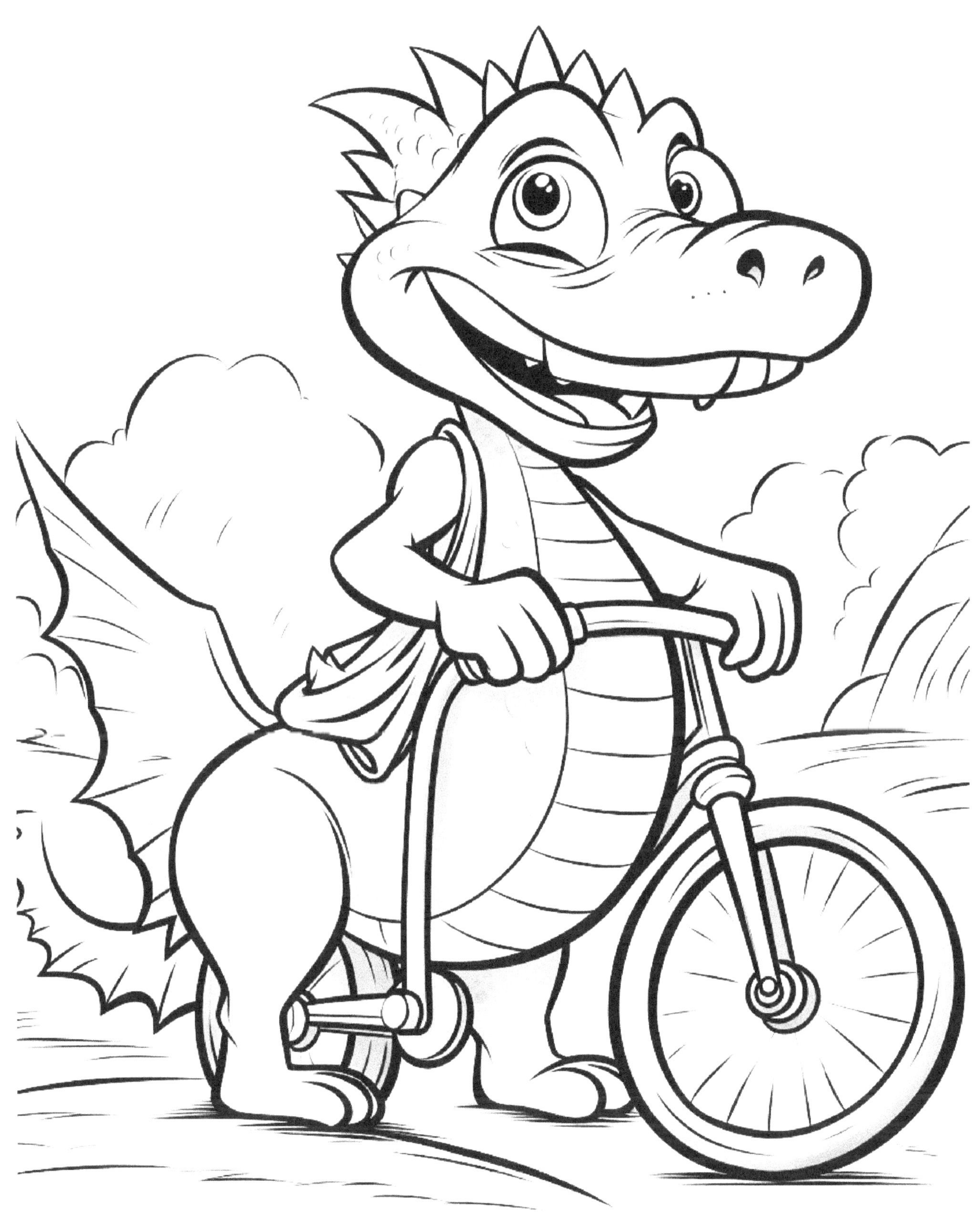

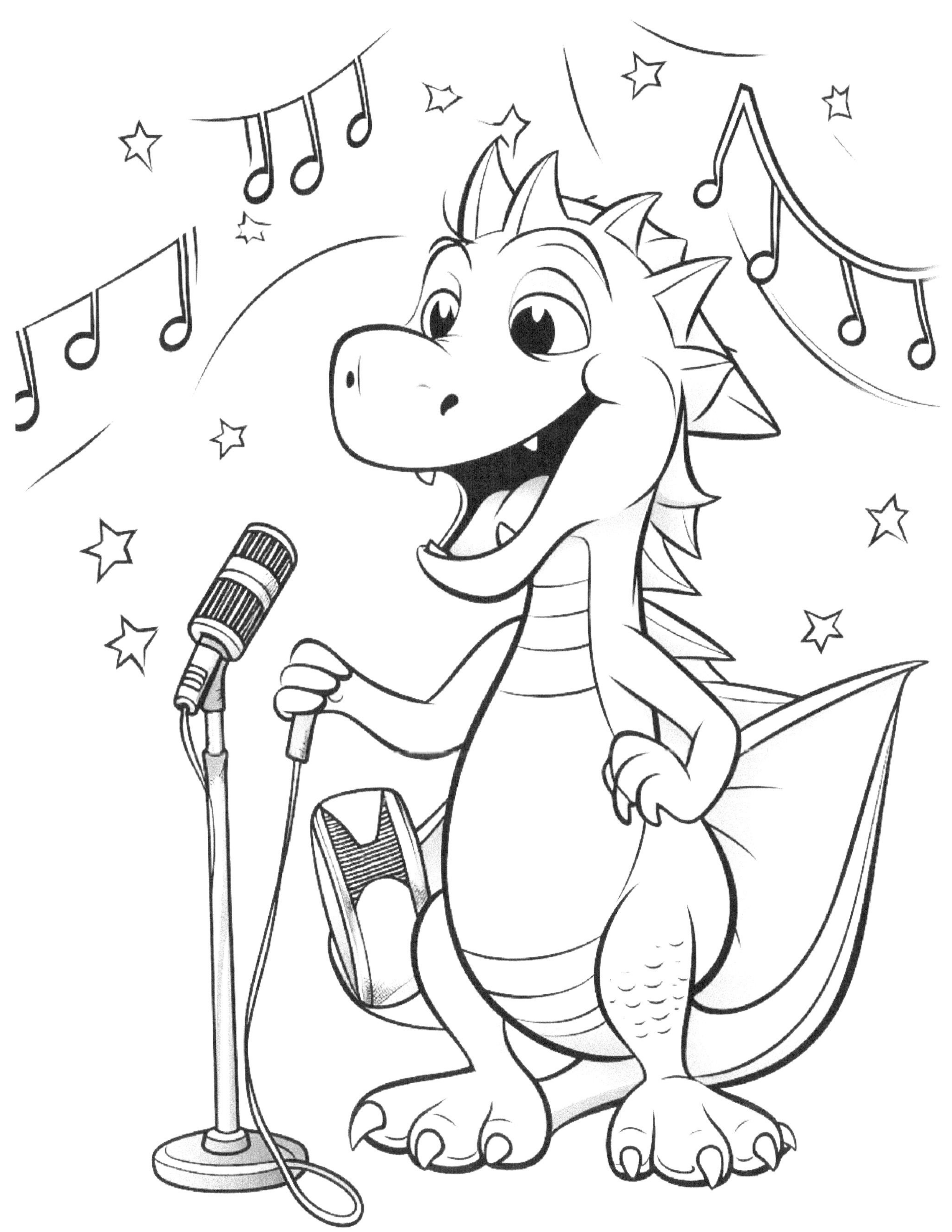

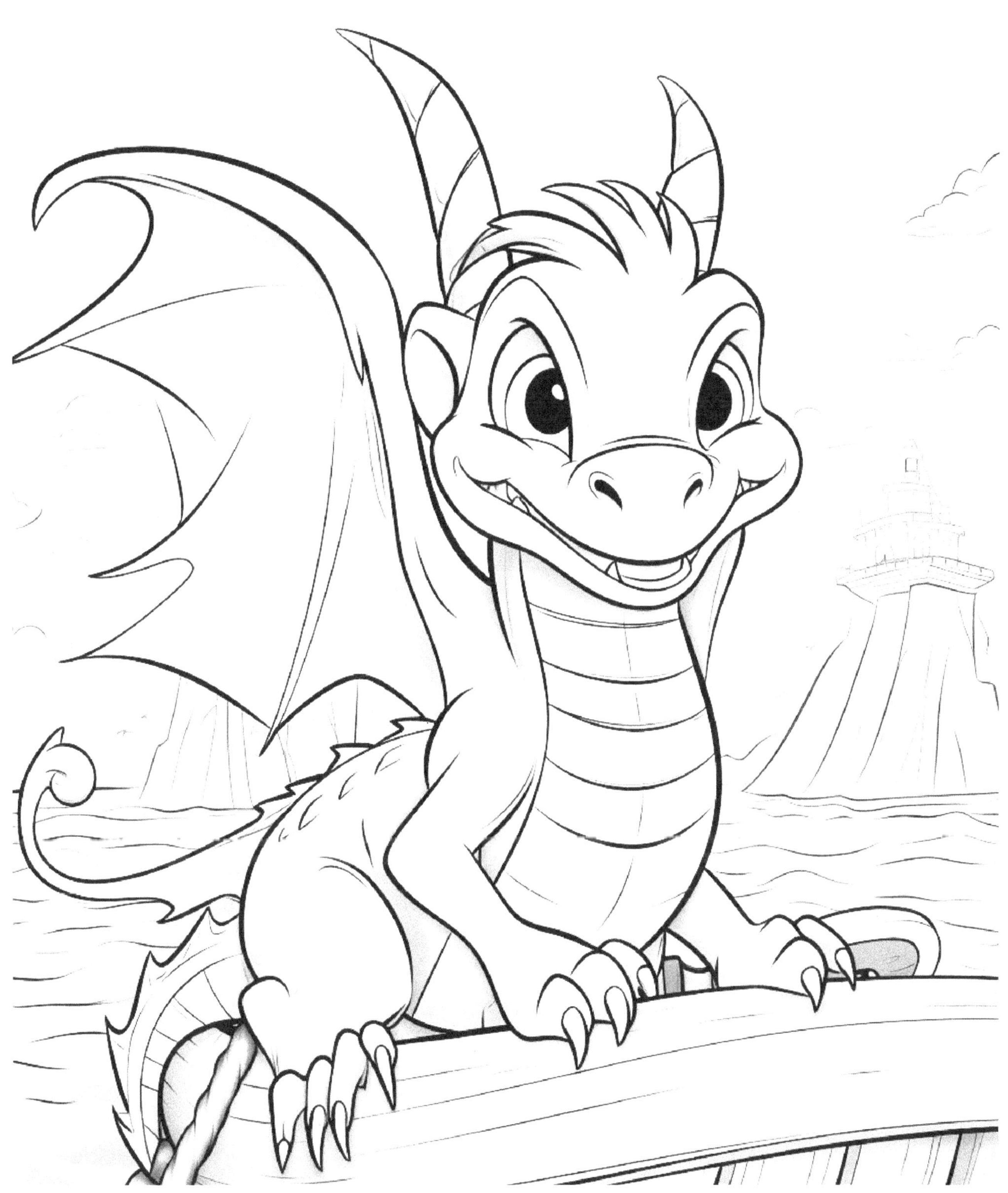

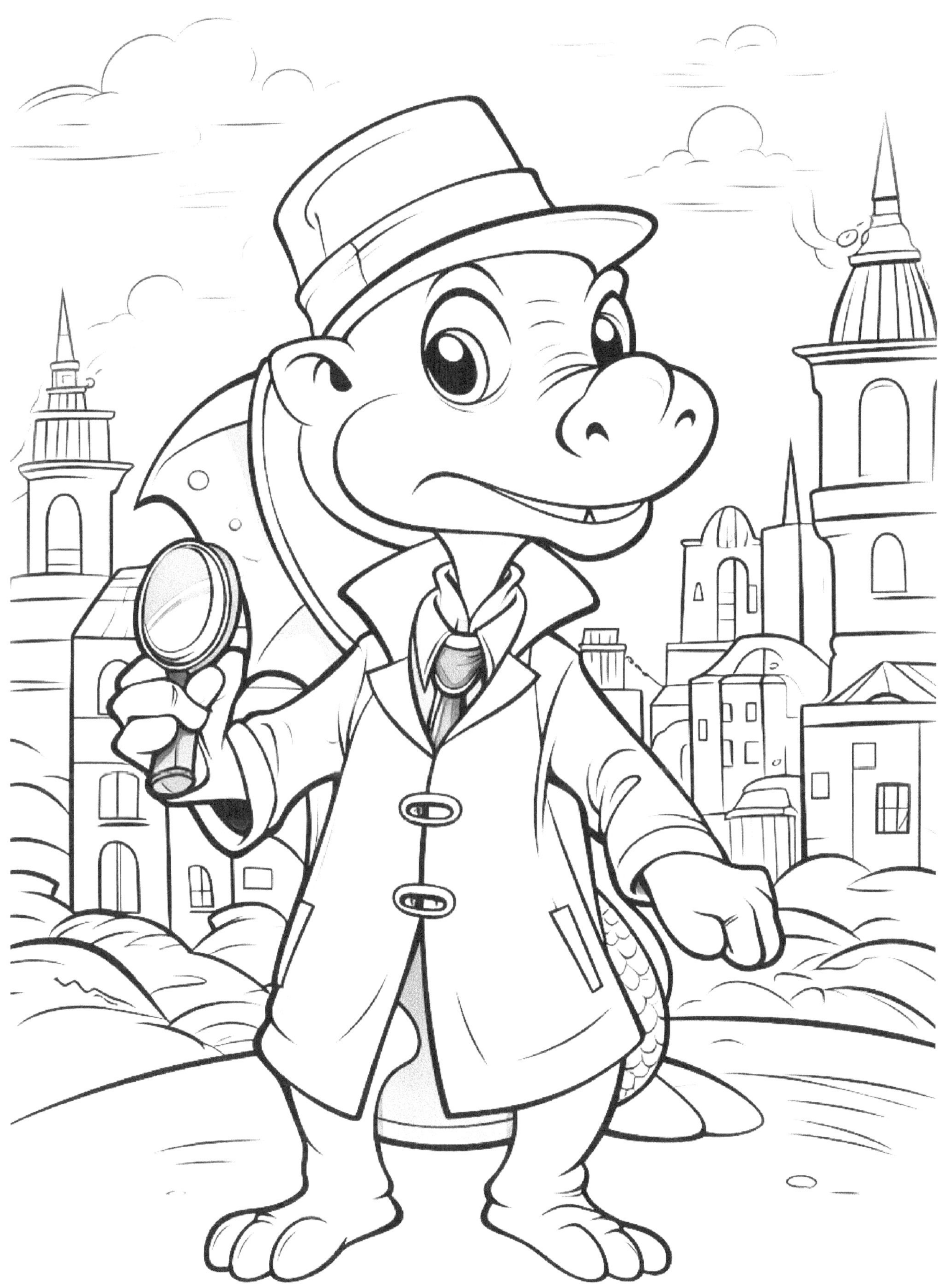

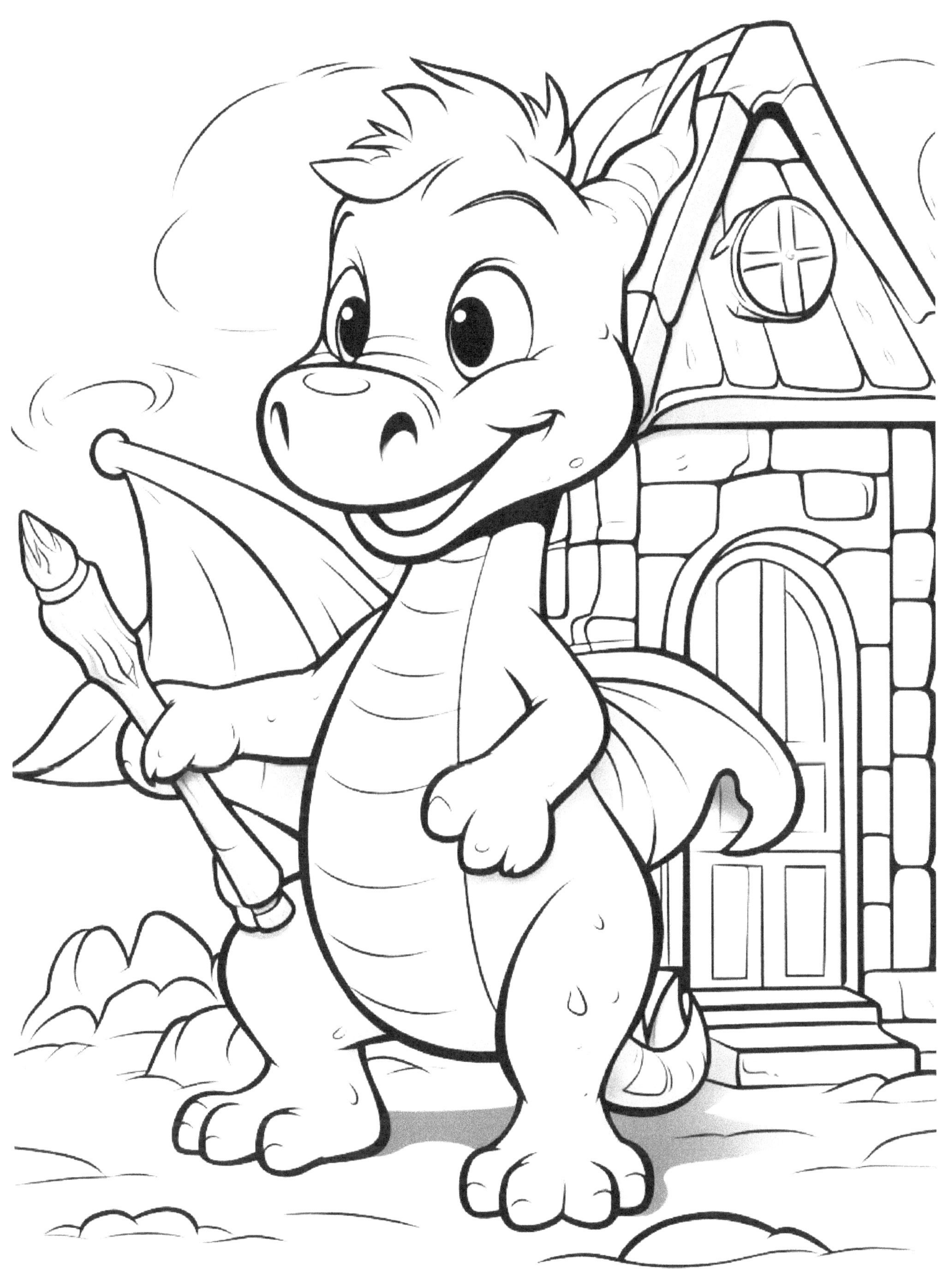

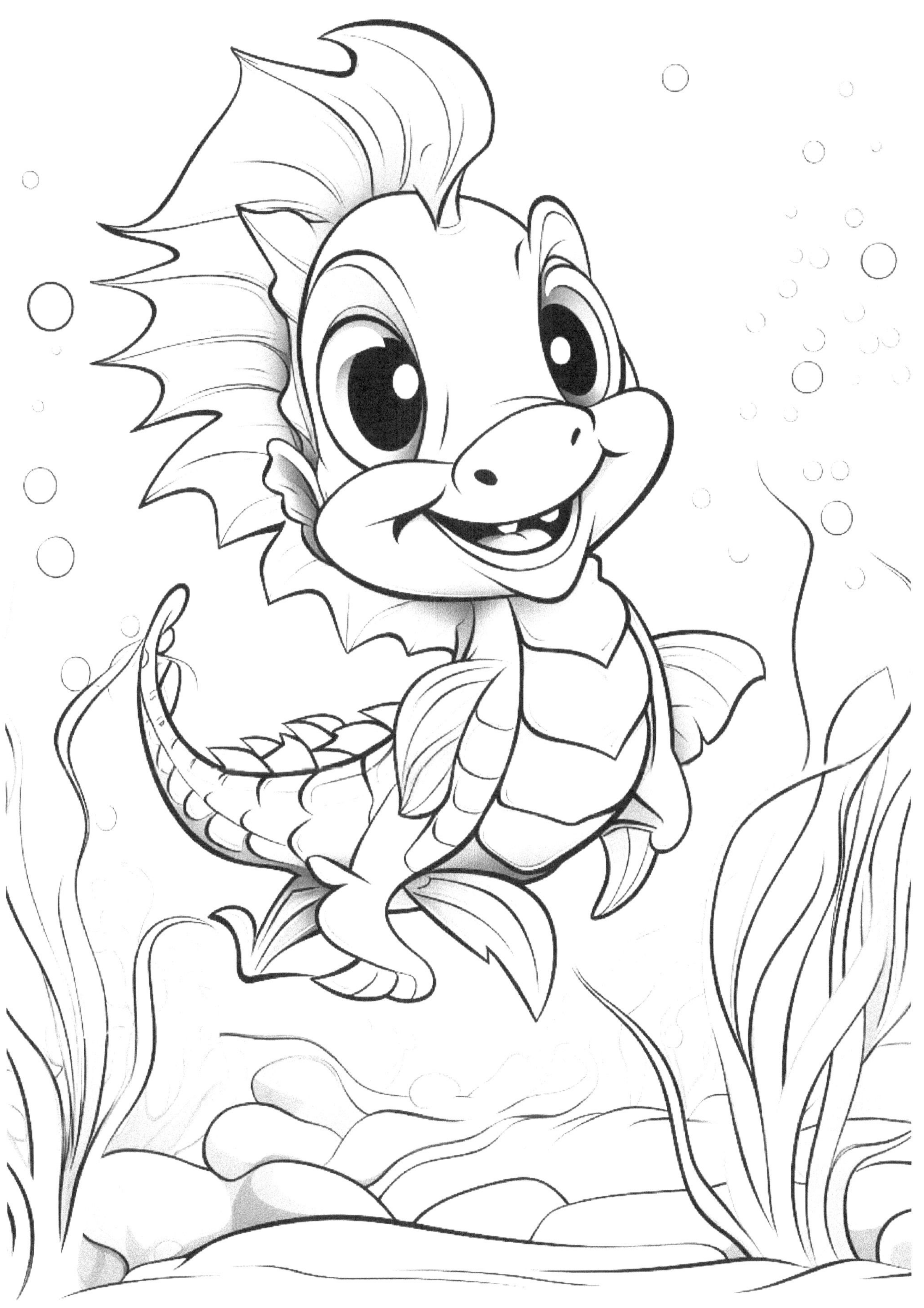

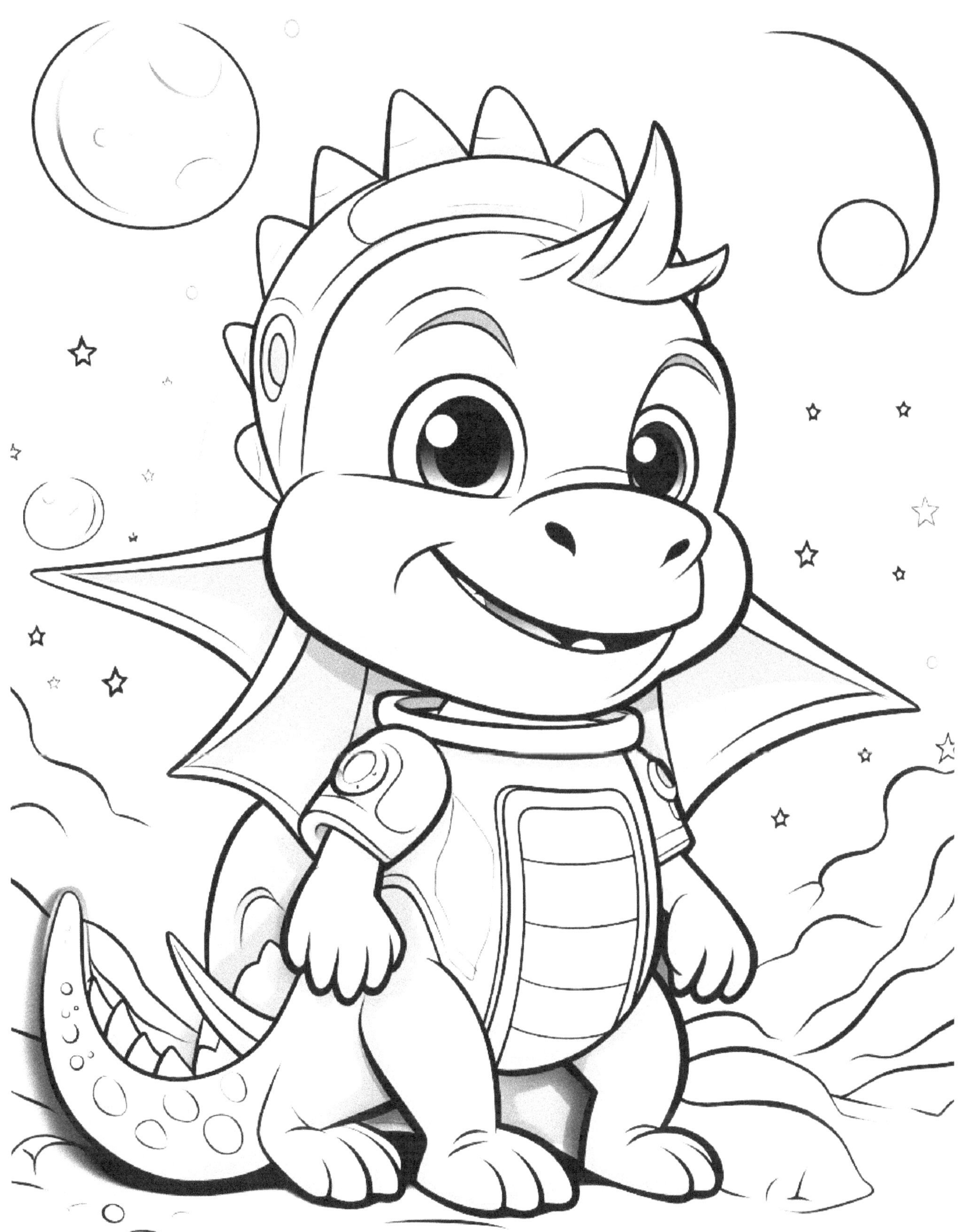

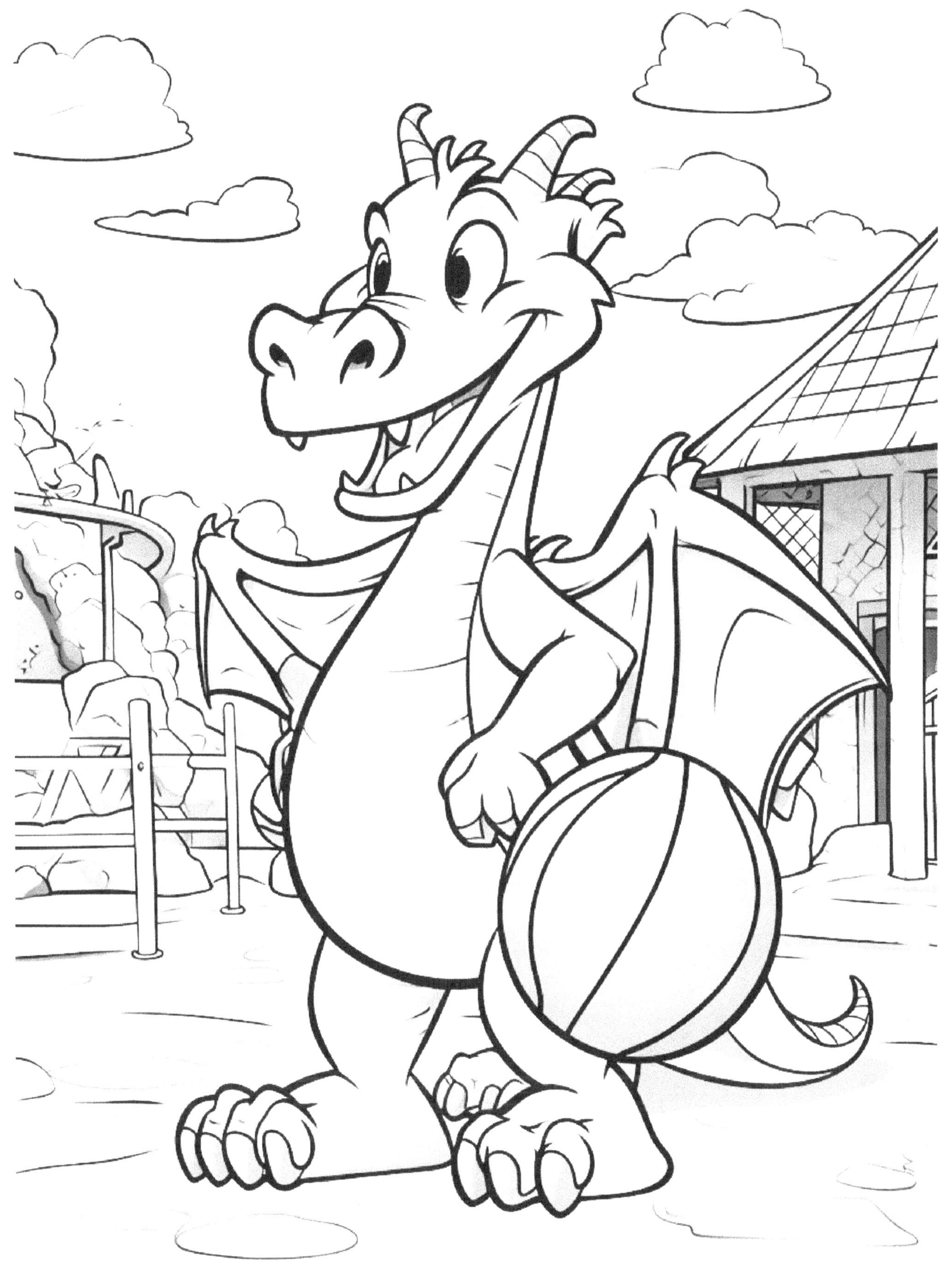

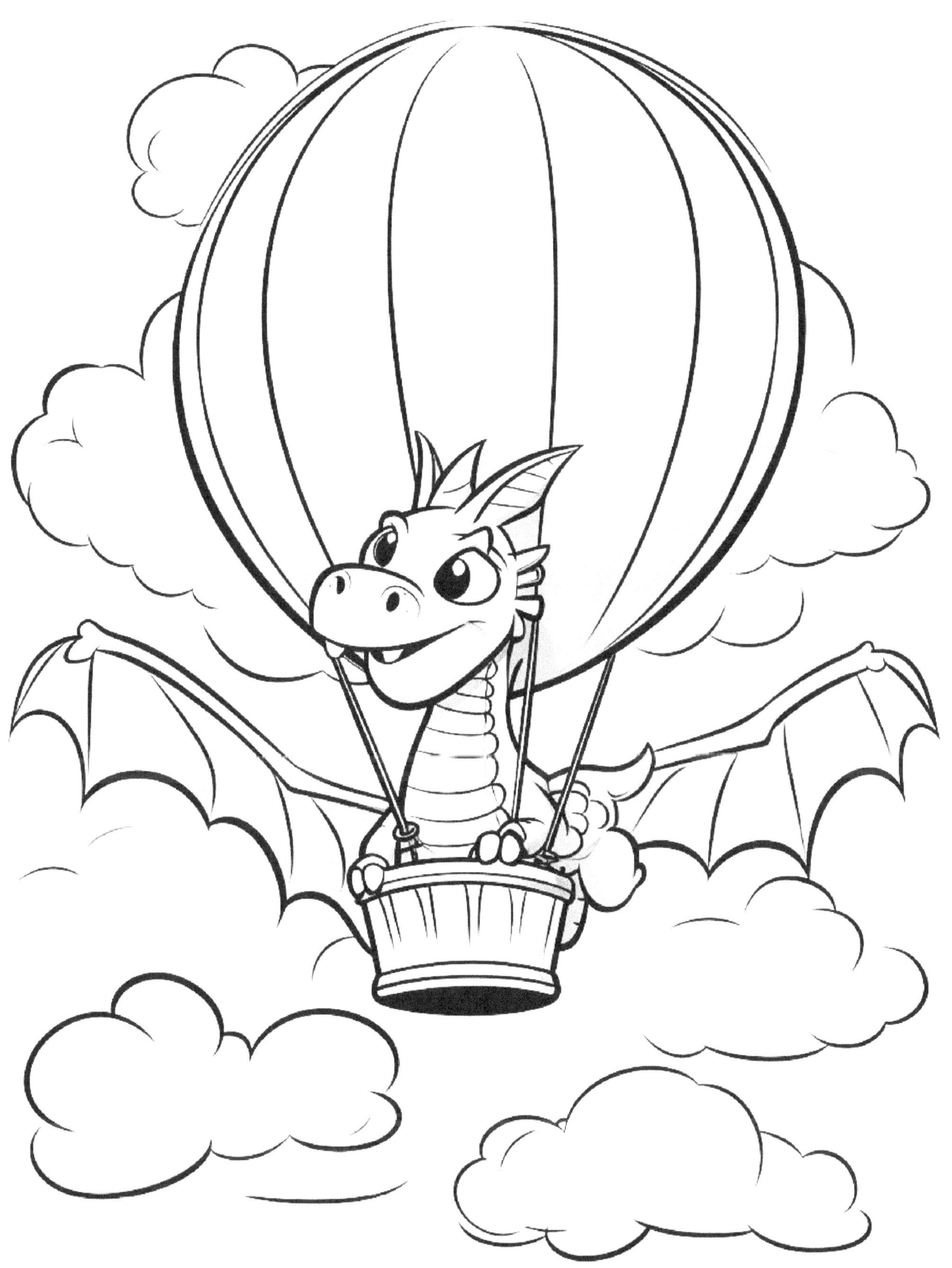

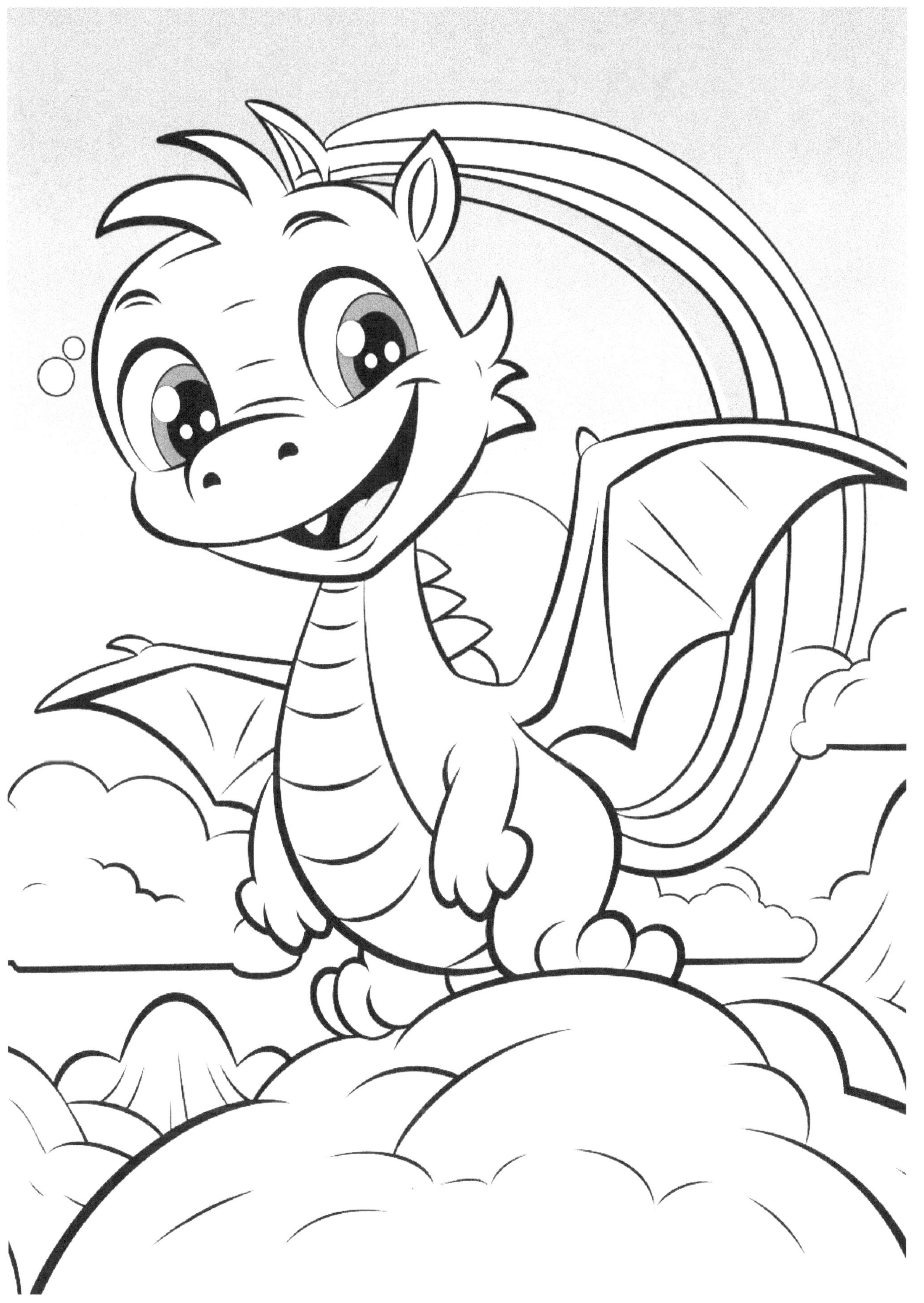

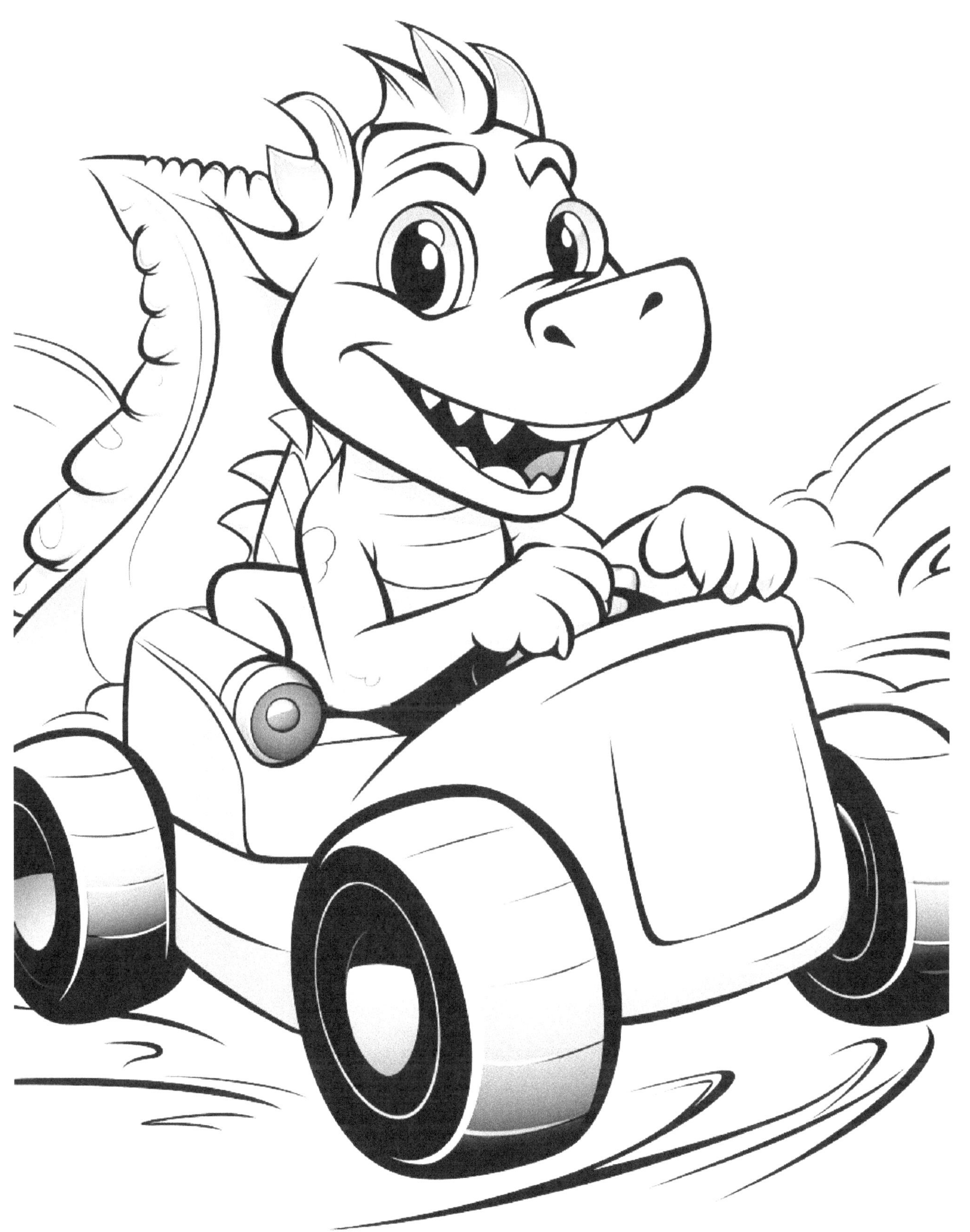